THE

LAZARUS

GENERATION

COME FORTH

THE

LAZARUS

GENERATION

COME FORTH

THE DEATH, BURIAL AND
RESURRECTION
OF YOUR DREAMS

VELMA CROW

TMN/WISDOM MERCHANTS PUBLISHING

TMN/Wisdom Merchants
admin@wisdommerchants.org
First Edition 2006
Second Edition 2012
Third Edition 2013

ISBN-13: 978-0615606040
ISBN-10: 0615606040

DEDICATION

This book is dedicated to anyone and everyone who ever had a dream to become, to do, to go, or any other God given desire. The gifts and calling of the Lord are irrevocable. Regardless your age, regardless your circumstance, whatever your hindrance, God is well able to enable you to overcome and step into the life and future He has ordained for you.

ENDORSEMENTS

Velma, it was very interesting reading your book. You did an excellent job of conveying your thoughts to the reader...I would love to have a copy to refer to (and one to give). It has so much to say...It really has wonderful material for reference on a continuing basis. The fact that you have written this shows how far you have progressed in healing and becoming "yourself" again.

Pat Reardon,
Fort Worth, Texas

THE SEMINAR WAS LIFE CHANGING! People lose the concept and need to be reminded of God's promises and that fulfillment in Him is their right as His children. This book will open doors for people to believe again.

Joyce Ross, Co-Pastor
Mineral Wells, Texas.

UNTIL I ATTENDED THIS SEMINAR I didn't understand the importance of my wife's desire to minister. On the way home, I apologized to her and asked her how I could help her pursue her call. I've continued to support her ever since that time in whatever God is telling her to do or become.

Knox Bruce.

THIS BOOK IS A MUST READ. It will awaken the buried destiny framed by your forgotten dreams and cause hope to spring forth into faith as it leads you into deeper development of godly character and healing of your soul. It is a timely, information highway through the valley of dead dreams to their resurrection and establishment in the community of Kingdom development. You will be inspired to stretch forth your withered dream, prophesying to those dead bones to live again infused with the breath of the Spirit of the Living God. THE LAZARUS GENERATION - COME FORTH will reignite the flame of desire and guide you to the full establishment of your divine call. It will cause you to be able to believe again.

Anonymous,
Benton, Illinois

"I HADN'T READ FAR in this wonderful compilation of God's word and study thereof when I realized this is speaking to ME! I thought, "How wonderful of my friend Velma to write a book just for ME!" " Yaaaaaaaaaay" as she would say with a smile as big as Texas. As I continued to digest the meat of this exciting adventure to resurrect my dreams (some buried in several layers of rejection, loss, grief and emotional pain), I soon realized not one of my dreams is really lost, dead, or unsalvageable. As I will continue to follow the guidelines to their resurrection, so marvelously based on God's word and His will in THE LAZARUS GENERATION, I have renewed hope, increased faith and joy unspeakable! This anointed work the Lord has given Velma to share with us, will place the Christian community on the plateaus our Heavenly Father intended all along. Happy Dream Resurrecting to all!"

Shirley J Parrish
President and Founder
My Father's House Christian Finishing School
Marion, Illinois

THIS TEACHING IS LIFE CHANGING, a rare combination of spiritual surgery and Holy Ghost healing, administered by Reverend Crow with that combination of skill and finesse that comes with maturing of an apostle. I was first introduced to this teaching through a seminar Reverend Crow presented concerning the death, burial and resurrection of your dreams. I knew this teaching was truly something special when my husband was in no hurry to leave. Even the noon meal we all shared was not the usual chatter but a chance to discuss what we had learned and the revelation we had gained. I don't think anyone left the same that day.

Pastor Cindy Bruce,
Mineral Wells, Texas

I first read THE LAZARUS GENERATION/Come Forth in 2005 after attending one of Rev. Velma Crow's speaking engagements in Southern Illinois. I said READ. I was comfortable, dreaming dreams, and wanted nothing more at that time. I laid it aside for years.

In 2011, devastated and depressed by circumstances beyond my immediate control, wrongly contemplating how nice to hurry myself to Heaven, not on earth any longer. God, through Rev. Crow, directed me to dream and not give in to the wiles of the evil one: through Lazarus Generation; to STUDY, not just read, the book. It is not a one-time-sit-down read. It is a slow study of how to acquire God's direction and one's dreams again; a book to be referenced again and again.

The second time I could not just read through - I had to stop and digest what I had read, to study each and every word this woman of God wrote. Rev. Crow is truly anointed, truly inspired to write what God wants said, and is able to put into words what each lost Child of God needs at a given moment. By all means, study this undertaking, get it, share it. See what

God is saying to each of us. He uses Rev. Crow to pull the truths from the Word and spread it abroad.

Praises to God and bless Rev. Crow for caring and daring. Lois Barrett, author, publisher, a Child of God.

Lois Barrett Brick Hill Publishing
barrett@brickhillpublishing.com
Author & Former Reporter
When The Earthquakes Spoke
Preacher's Son & Henry Brown
There Oughta Be A Law
Gulf Coast Love Affair
www.brickhillpublishing.com

THIS BOOK IS WONDERFUL!   *What I like about it is that it's* to the point. It's well related between the Bible and her personal experience. Velma clearly shows how the Bible is Living Word that when applied to our present day lives can carry us to victorious living.

Pastor Ethel Severin
Fires of Revival, Benton, Illinois

CONTENTS

Acknowledgments

Introduction
Preface

ACKNOWLEDGMENTS

I AM SO BLESSED!

Heartfelt "Thank YOU" go to Emma Moore and Crystal Medina for their assistance in editing this manuscript for its third printing. Your help was invaluable and I appreciate the time and effort you put into it.

My deep gratitude to Pat Reardon whom God uses to ignite His timing in my life. Thank you for sensing the urging of Holy Spirit to speak into my life. You understand the times and seasons. Thank you also for your editing and proofreading skills as well as your continual encouragement. You are a faithful friend.

Thank you and may God mightily bless all of you on whom He has placed a burden to intercede on my behalf. You are my right foot to success in my call and assignments. Thank you for hearing Him and covering me with your prayers.

INTRODUCTION

The gifts and callings of God are irrevocable ^{Romans 11:29}.

- If it wasn't too late for Abraham at 100, Moses at 80 or Caleb at 86, then it isn't too late for you.
- Motherhood nor wifely duties kept Deborah from becoming the only woman recorded in the Bible to rule as judge over Israel and lead their armies next to Barak.
- Being an orphan, not royal blood and raised in a completely different culture than that of the ruling kingdom, did not keep Esther out of the palace, nor did it prevent her from fulfilling God's call on her life, preserving the nation of Israel.
- Being raised in a dysfunctional family, betrayed by his brothers and serving time in prison did not keep Joseph from becoming chief in the land, second only to Pharaoh.
- Harlotry did not keep Rahab out of the lineage of Jesus, The Christ.
- Being a foreigner and Moabite (pagan) princess could not prevent Ruth from becoming the grandmother of the great King David thus winning her a place in Christ's lineage.
- David had the nerve to believe the words of the prophet qualified him to move from herding sheep to become the commander of a great army then step from the back of a horse onto the throne.
- Having a really bad reputation with the church did not prevent Saul of Tarsus from becoming one of the most renowned Christian leaders of all time, writing a third of the New Testament and establishing many churches in gentile nations because he was a chosen vessel of the Lord.
- Being pregnant out of wedlock, for which the reward in that day was to be stoned to death, did not prevent

a young woman named Mary from carrying her baby full term, giving birth to the Savior of the world.

- Being raised a carpenter did not prevent Jesus from getting to know God as His Father, walking on water, casting out devils, raising the dead, and living a sinless life though tempted with every temptation common to man, guarding His blood so it would be a fit sacrifice for reconciliation between God and mankind and redeeming the earth from the power of the devil.

Look at the great men and women of today: Martin Luther King, Oral Roberts, Mary Kay Ash, Smith Wigglesworth, Bill Gates, Chuck Pierce, Ronald Reagan, Condoleezza Rice, Benjamin Netanyahu, Barbara Wentroble, Kenneth and Gloria Copeland, Pat Robertson, Dutch Sheets, Oprah Winfrey, Kenneth Hagin, T. D. Jakes, David Younggi Cho, Albert Einstein, Warren Buffett, Maya Angelou, Nikola Tesla, Colin Powell, countless others—astronauts, inventors, authors, athletes, government leaders, soldiers, housewives. No. They are not all devout Christians but they all had a dream, a goal, and a road of circumstances and obstacles to overcome. They all had a destiny—a God given purpose that changed the world for the better. You say, "They didn't have the same obstacles I do. My circumstances are much worse." I know. No one did and they always are. Nor did you face their obstacles or live under their circumstances.

Look again. You'll find you're living someone else's story. It may be someone who went before you, or perhaps, someone who will come after. You may be paving the way for the next generation. What legacy will you leave?

Our loving Father gives us the desires of our heart. He instills desires within our hearts so He can bring them forth as we follow His road to success. No, it won't be easy but it will build strong character. No, you can't do it alone so you'll have to learn to lean on Him, trusting Him in all things. It won't be popular. You'll have to leave some friends behind, maybe even some family members so you can embrace others who believe in you. So, dust off those dreams and promises. Let hope spring up in your heart, for hope is the key that unlocks faith.

If you are not on speaking terms with God—Father Son and Holy Spirit—earnestly pray the prayer below trusting Him to hear you and reveal Himself to you as you work through this book.

Oh, Jesus,
Son of the Living God,
I know God's plan for me is bigger than my ability.
I also know I have made many mistakes and have even
sinned against
God and man.
Please forgive me of all these things.
Deliver me from myself and anything that hinders me.
Please come, make your home in my heart, my inner man,
my soul.
I submit myself to you and ask you to be
my Lord and King of my life.

If you decide to embrace your dreams, heeding the call of God, you have taken the first step to resurrection. You are now a member of The Lazarus Generation—a company of people who are willing to say, "Dream! Vision! Promise! COME FORTH!"

Preface
IN THE BEGINNING

"The beginning of Wisdom is: get Wisdom (skillful and godly Wisdom)!
[For skillful and godly Wisdom is the principal thing.]
And with all you have gotten,
get understanding
(discernment, comprehension, and interpretation) ^{Proverbs 4:7}.

The first thing we want to do is gain wisdom and understanding of the following scripture, Hebrews 11:1. For me, the above scripture, Proverbs 4:7 and the following scripture, Hebrews 11:1, are the corner stones of our foundations for success in life, both spiritual and natural life. I also believe that Salvation through Jesus Christ who is the Chief Corner Stone is the most important, the main principal thing. However, without Wisdom and understanding many people "fall away," not moving from the experience to the working out of salvation—often not knowing they needed to.

*Now **FAITH** is the **SUBSTANCE** of things **HOPED** for*
*The **EVIDENCE** of things not seen.*
Hebrews 11:1

Let's look at some of these words:
- There may be a few surprises here for some of you. There was for me.

FAITH

4102 pistis {pis'-tis} Greek: noun feminine from 3982;
Possible Definitions:

1) conviction of the truth of anything, belief; in the NT of a conviction or belief respecting man's relationship to God and divine things, generally with the included idea of trust and holy fervour born of faith and joined with it

The root word, Strong's #3982, is interesting. Among other things it means:

2b) to listen to, obey, yield to, comply with

3) to trust, have confidence, be confident

SUBSTANCE

5287 hupostasis {hoop-os'-tas-is} Greek: noun feminine from a compound of 5259 and 2476;
Possible Definitions:

1) a setting or placing under; thing put under, substructure, foundation

2) that which has foundation, is firm; hence
   2a) that which has actual existence; a substance, real being
   2b) the substantial quality, nature, of a person or thing
   2c) the steadfastness of mind, firmness, courage, resolution;
       confidence, firm trust, assurance

THINGS

4229 pragma {prag'-mah} Greek: noun neuter from 4238;
Possible Definitions:

1a) that which has been done, a deed, an accomplished fact

1b) what is done or being accomplished; spec. business, a commercial transaction

1c) a matter, question, affair; spec. in a forensic sense, a matter at law, case, suit

1d) that which is or exists, a thing

HOPED

1679 elpizo {el-pid'-zo} Greek: verb from 1680;
Possible Definitions:

1) to hope (in a religious sense, to wait for salvation with joy and full confidence), hopefully to trust in

EVIDENCE

1650 elegchos {el'-eng-khos} Greek: noun masculine from 1651;
Possible Definitions:

1) a proof, that by which a thing is proved or tested
2) conviction

BUT NOTICE

It takes hope to build faith.

Faith works by Love.

*You shall love the Lord your God
with all your heart and with all your soul
and with all your mind (intellect).
This is the great (most important, principal) and first
commandment.*

Matthew 22:37-38

(There's a whole chapter about Love!)

Let's take a look at the progress of faith.

First we hope.

Then we evaluate ourselves and find scripture to base our hope on and begin to believe based on our knowledge of ourselves and understanding of scripture. We add prophetic words we have received. We begin to believe this thing could come to pass.

Often in the Bible, the word translated "believe" is the same word translated as "faith"

So FAITH is born.

If what we're believing for doesn't come to pass when we think it should – in our time - we soon step out of faith and begin hoping again.

When hope is gone we turn to wishing.

When we're "wishing" basically, our dream is dead. Because wishing won't prompt us to step out with the hope that we can do that thing so we don't develop faith that it will come to pass.

WE MUST HAVE HOPE

On the basis of Hope, we can build Faith.
Faith is the confidence of the truth of a thing.
Even the conviction of what cannot yet be seen.

CHAPTER 1
MY DREAM IS DEAD–WHAT NOW?

"Life will happen to you at random
if you don't exercise the gift of CHOICE.
Godly character is built on informed, godly choices."

If you have chosen to read this book, you, at the very least, think you may have a divine purpose to fulfill or you have a dream or a promise from the Lord for a future with an expected end.

Perhaps that purpose is embedded in ministry—preaching, teaching, singing, making music, praying.

Perhaps your heart's desire is to invent, to write, to build a business.

It may be that your dream is to somehow make a difference in third world countries—improve living conditions, drill water wells, teach living skills such as how to plant and harvest a garden, even provide them with knowledge to live above the norm, or perhaps you simply want get to know the people of that land.

1

Do you desire to write books or do you have songs within you crying out to be sung?

Do you long to design clothes, houses, churches, public buildings or roads—anything?

Do you have great and lofty desires or simple, serving urges? Sometimes the most simple things are given the highest honor by our Lord ^{Matthew 23:11}.

Maybe you've actually drawn up blueprints for your dream. Perhaps you've collected materials for…when…and…if.

Do you know what your call or assignment is? Do you understand the promise? If you don't yet know or understand, take a close look at your heart. What gives you joy? When are you the most fulfilled—the most satisfied? What riles you, gets your dander up, makes you angry? Is there anything you can do about it? Have you even considered doing something about it—making a change? If you were given an all expense paid year to live your dream or promise, what would you do? How would you start?

Did you have a dream, a vision, a promise for your life but now you assume it's out of reach or its time has passed? Did you choose another road, a road that led you away from your dream? Perhaps the road you chose once led you to fulfillment but now circumstances are different and you wonder, "What if?"

- What if I was younger?
- What if I didn't have kids?
- What if I wasn't married? What if I was?
- What if I were older?
- What if I had chosen differently?

2

- What if I had incorporated my dreams so two roads came together?
- What if I had done something else first?
- What if I do something else now?
- What if?!

Are you living your dream right now but still lack that sense of fulfillment or completeness? Does it seem as though there is something more but you can't quite put your finger on it? Are you ready for the next phase but you're not exactly sure what the next phase is or how to get there? This book may hold some answers for you.

Is your dream completely dead or at the very least, extremely weak? If so, it may be time for a resurrection:
- A resurrection of hope.
- A resurrection of desire.
- A resurrection of vision.

It's time to look at your dream, your vision, your promise from the perspective of where you are now. It's time to get past your past, evaluate your present and look into your future. It isn't too late. Even if you're dragging your dream around knowing full well it's dead and there is nothing you can do about it, He still can. The gifts and callings of the Lord are irrevocable [Romans 11:29]. If He put that desire in your heart, with your cooperation, He will bring it to pass [Psalm 37:4-5]. It may not look like it would have years and experiences ago, but remember, you are a member of The Lazarus Generation.

First things first—there are qualifications for fulfillment.

- Character issues must be dealt with.
- Erroneous beliefs must be corrected.
- Good habits must be formed and bad habits abandoned.
- Some generational issues have to be overcome; others may need to be embraced.

Our lives must be lived on purpose and with focus. The "come what may" attitude won't get you to your destination. Without purpose you can't develop focus. Without focus you can't see your destination. You must have a goal and an end in sight. If you can see the end from the beginning, you will be able to count the cost, make adjustments, take the right road and avoid detours ^{Luke 14:28}.

The death of a thing does not have to be the end unless:
- We actually are unwilling to hope.
- Or, if we do nothing while that thing is in the grave.

We often hear or read of people who were divorced decades ago and remarry in their latter years. You may know someone who married their childhood sweetheart in their old age. Many people build a business after they retire. So the death of a thing may actually mean rebirth—rebirth of the original desire or birth of success in another area.

Let's take our lead from Jesus. Sometimes a thing has to die so God can be glorified. John, Chapter 11 relates the account of Lazarus dying and being raised from the dead after four days. A messenger was sent to tell Jesus His good friend, Lazarus, was very ill. It was a day's journey from Lazarus' home in Bethany to where Jesus was staying. He could have sent the Word of healing. He had done that before Matthew 8:5-13; 15:22-28; Mark 7:24-30; Luke 7:2-10; John 4:46-53. He could have gone to Bethany and touched him. But, He chose to wait a couple of days. He purposely waited until He knew by the Spirit that Lazarus was dead before He began the day's journey to Bethany. He did tell the messenger that this sickness was not to end in death but was rather to honor God and promote His glory so the Son of God would be glorified John 11:4-7.

Let's take a closer look at this account from the eleventh chapter of John.

When Jesus received the message (that Lazarus was sick) He said, "This sickness is not to end in death; but on the contrary, it is to honor God and to promote His glory that the Son of God may be glorified through (by) it John 11:4.

Oh! But—Lazarus did die. Even so—death was not the end.

Jesus knew Lazarus was going to die. Just so, when He put that dream in your heart, He knew it would die. He knew He would have to raise it from the dead. You have to know He can.

Look what happened next, two days later. Jesus knew it was time to visit Lazarus.

Then Jesus told them plainly, "Lazarus is dead, and for your sake I am glad that I was not there; it will

5

help you to believe (to trust and rely on Me).
However, let us go to him" ^{John 11:14-15}.

You see what happened here and how it relates to your dream? When Lazarus was beyond human help, here came Jesus. When your dream is beyond anything you can do to bring it to pass, go to Jesus. "Lord, my Lazarus (my dream) is dead." Acknowledge your need of help. Ask Him for His input. Your dream dies to the image of your plan and is resurrected in the image of God's plan for it and for you. So, stretch forth that withered dream so He can touch it.

O.K. Let's see what Martha and Mary actually thought about Jesus' delayed arrival. What were they believing? Was there *any* hope left? They knew that Jesus could raise their brother—if He wanted to. He had raised other people from the dead ^{Matthew 9:18-25; Mark 5:35-42; Luke 7:11-15; Luke 8:41-55}; but Lazarus had already begun to deteriorate. Still, you can hear the hope though their faith was gone.

When Martha heard that Jesus was coming, she went
to meet Him, while Mary remained sitting in the
house. Martha then said to Jesus, "Master, if You had
been here, my brother would not have died. And even
now I know that whatever You ask from God, He will
grant it to You" ^{John 11:20-22}.

You see? Martha knew it wasn't too late though logic and fact said it was. Logic said, "He's dead, In fact, he's deteriorating and probably wormy by now." But she said,

6

"Even now, whatever you ask, God will do." Let's look a little further.

Jesus said to her, "Your brother shall rise again" ^{John 11:23}.

Ah! The promise!
Martha replied, "I know that he will rise again in the resurrection at the last day" ^{John 11:24}.

Like Martha we often misunderstand or misinterpret the promise and its timing.

Jesus said to her, "I Am (Myself) the Resurrection and the Life. Whoever believes in (adheres to, trusts in, and relies on) Me, although he may die, yet he shall live; and whoever continues to live and believes in (has faith in, cleaves to, and relies on) Me shall never actually die at all. Do you believe this?" ^{John 11:25-26}.

She said to Him, "Yes, Lord, I have believed (I do believe) that You are the Christ (the Messiah, the Anointed One), the Son of God, even He Who was to come into the world. [It is for your coming that the world has waited.] ^{John 11:27}.

Notice here, Martha is dealing with facts. "I know that he shall rise again in the resurrection at the last day." That is a fact but TRUTH is standing right in front of her! Truth has just said, "I Am The Resurrection." We often struggle in this same way. We know what the Lord has told us about a situation but we continue looking at the facts and are tempted to embrace them rather than holding on to the truth He has planted in our hearts.

FACT is not a sure foundation! TRUTH is! How many times have we heard a doctor proclaim fact that someone would die then see TRUTH make the difference and the person live? By His stripes/wounds we are healed ^{Isaiah 53:5; I Peter 2:24}!

How many court cases have been reversed because TRUTH carried more weight than fact? People in the wrong place at the wrong time—facts speaking loudly, "Guilty." Then D.N.A., a truth setter declares, "Not Guilty." How many marriages have been saved because TRUTH was given place in hopeless situations? How many dead dreams have been revived because TRUTH awakened in us hope and hope gave birth to faith? Then by the substance of faith, the dream came forth.

Continuing on with Lazarus, let's look at John 11:32-38:
When Mary came to the place where Jesus was and saw Him, she dropped down at His feet, saying to Him, "Lord, if You had been here, my brother would not have died."
When Jesus saw her sobbing, and the Jews who came with her also sobbing, He was deeply moved in spirit and troubled. [He chafed in spirit and sighed and was disturbed.] And He said, "Where have you laid him?"
They said to Him, "Lord, come and see." Jesus wept. The Jews said, "See how tenderly He loved him!" but

some of them said, "Could not He who opened a blind man's eyes have prevented this man from dying?" Now Jesus, again sighing repeatedly and deeply disquieted, approached the tomb. It was a cave (a hole in the rock). And a boulder lay against the entrance to close it.

As you can see, the Jews started criticizing Jesus. Be assured, some of your friends and relatives will criticize you when you begin standing on your promise concerning the dream in your heart. That word "sighing" in the above scripture is translated "groaning" in the King James and is a compound Greek word which also means "to snort in anger" strong's #1690. When people say "Did God really say," and belittle us because of our faith, I believe it makes the Lord angry. Didn't He ask Saul of Tarsus, *"Saul, Saul, why are you persecuting ME [harassing, troubling, and molesting ME]?* And Saul who thought he was persecuting the church said, *"Who are You, Lord?"* Then the Lord said, *"I am Jesus whom you are persecuting"* Acts 9:3-5. We are His body. When someone comes against us they are actually coming against Jesus, Himself. We need to pray for mercy and that they be shown TRUTH as these Jews are about to see at Lazarus' tomb. Look at John 11:39-40:

Jesus said, "Take away the stone."
Martha, the sister of the dead man, exclaimed, "But Lord, by this time he is decaying and throws off an offensive odor, for he has been dead four days!"

Jesus said to her, "Did I not tell you and promise you that if you would believe and rely on Me, you would see the glory of God?"

Can you identify with Martha here? She has hope in her heart but she's still looking at the facts. Unlike the Shunammite woman in 2 Kings, chapter 4, who, when her son died would only say, "It is well," refusing to profess the fact that her child was dead even when asked directly, "Is it well with the child?"

None of you reading this book may ever look at facts while the TRUTH is speaking in your ears, but I sometimes do. Sometimes I have a lot of questions. I often ask things like:

- Lord, I know what You said, but did You really mean what I perceived You to say or do I need to look at it from another angle?
- Did I misinterpret what you said?
- Did I make what you said look like my desire?"

Friends, that's called doubt. Being double-minded. We can't waiver between two opinions. That cripples us. James 1:6-8 says, *"...it must be in faith that he asks with no wavering (no hesitating, no doubting). For the one who wavers (hesitates, doubts) is like the billowing surge out at sea that is blown hither and thither and tossed by the wind. For truly, let not such a person imagine that he will receive anything [he asks for] from the Lord, [For being as he is] a man of two minds (hesitating, dubious, irresolute), [he is] unstable and unreliable and uncertain about everything [he*

10

thinks, feels, decides]." James 4:8 tells us that the cure for double-mindedness is to purify our hearts.

Please understand. I'm not suggesting in any way that we should not get confirmation of what we hear or what we believe. There is nothing wrong with setting a "fleece" as Gideon or asking for a sign as Abram and several others in the Bible did. "Lord, what sign will you give me that I've heard You and You will do it?" But once we receive confirmation or clarification, we should begin walking in that assurance and building our faith that what God has shown us or spoken to us will come to pass rather than continually asking for confirmation after confirmation. As our faith and confidence in the Lord begin to grow we won't have to ask for a sign of assurance.

I once received a word from the Lord that was monumental in my life, but I was unable to reach past woundedness to embrace it. I didn't ask for confirmation but the Lord sent me to a friend with whom I did not want to visit at the time. The Lord wouldn't let me pass her work place. He kept saying, "Stop by and see her."

I kept saying, "Lord, I'm tired." "I don't want to see her today." (I didn't know He had confirmation on His mind! However, it should have been enough that He asked me to stop.)

I had been to Oklahoma City and was driving back to Fort Worth. A few miles before the exit that would take me by the business where my friend worked, the Lord began, again, dealing with me to stop in and see her. Finally, just as I reached the exit, I said, "O.K.! O.K.! I'll stop and see her!"

This word from the Lord was so fresh and of such a personal nature that I would not have shared it with anyone without specific direction from the Lord even had I embraced it. Within minutes of our greeting, her face turned from soft and friendly to a look of shock and she staggered back a couple of steps, then spoke the very thing the Lord had put in my spirit.

I said, "Say that again!?" In one phrase I was both demanding she speak it again and asking if she had said what I heard. The thing she had spoken was crystal clear. She not only spoke the event, she named names that had never been connected with me but were crucial to the fulfillment. By this time her mouth, which had dropped open when the revelation was deposited in her mind by the Lord, was now closed, sealed. Her eyes were still quite large with surprise. She would not speak it again. She wouldn't say anything. She just looked at me with that surprise on her face.

The Lord could not have not have given a more clear or strong confirmation of promise and purpose even though I was not sure I wanted to believe, let alone embrace it. There was no room for doubt concerning His plan for this life-changing event. Yet, I spent years asking for confirmation after confirmation. That was living in doubt. He is so patient and tolerant. Time after time after time after time, the Lord responded to my need of confirmation. At last, I became able to embrace, even desire and pursue what was spoken though I often reminded Him it was not my idea. There does come a time when He will say, "Enough is enough!" He stopped striving with the Children of Israel. He may stop striving with us if we are unwilling to embrace the future and purpose He has for planned for us.

If we set our hearts to hear God concerning a specific matter, we need to know He will answer the question in our heart. He won't give us a serpent when we ask for an egg ^{Luke 11:12}.

Now, getting back to Lazarus.

So they took away the stone, and Jesus lifted up His eyes and said, "Father, I thank You that You have heard Me. Yes, I know You always hear and listen to Me, but I have said this on account of and for the benefit of the people standing around, so that they may believe that You did send Me [that You have made Me Your Messenger]." When He had said this, He shouted with a loud voice, "LAZARUS, COME OUT!" And out walked the man who had been dead, his hands and feet wrapped in burial cloths (linen strips), and with a burial napkin bound around his face. Jesus said to them, "Free him of the burial wrappings and let him go." ^{John 11:41-44}.

Jesus waited until Lazarus had been dead and in the grave four days. He was stinking! No one could say he wasn't dead or that he was in a coma. He was already deteriorating. The FACT was—Lazarus was dead. Even then at the Word of TRUTH, "Lazarus Come Forth," Lazarus came out of that grave! If it can happen for a physical body that has already begun deteriorating, it can certainly happen for your dream.

Stretch out your hope! Let faith be reborn, then feed your faith with action.

Let's look at another incident, Jesus' own time in the grave. We don't know what Lazarus did while he was in the grave, but we do know at least some of what Jesus did. He was pretty busy! He picked up the keys to hell and death ^{Revelation 1:18}. (In 1 Corinthians 15:55 referred to as death and the grave. Also see Hosea 13:14.)

- o Keys denote authority and power - Strong's #2807.
  - The root of which is #2808 and means to obstruct the entrance into the kingdom of heaven.

Our God given dreams, God's plans for our lives, are designed to establish His Kingdom on earth. The kingdom of God is within us ^{Luke 17:21}. There are keys to unlock those plans so they can be established.

- There are also qualifications to get the keys.
  - o We have to have ears to hear what the Father is saying ^{Matthew 11:15; chapter 13; Mark 4:9, 24-25; 7:14,16; Luke 8:18; 14:35; Revelation 2&3}.
  - o We must have the character to do what we hear ^{Matthew 21:28-31; 25:1-13; 14-30; Luke 19:12-27}.
  - o And we must be in agreement with someone ^{Matthew 16:18-19; 18:18-20}.

Back to Jesus while His body was in the grave:
- He preached to the spirits in prison even those who were destroyed in the flood of Noah ^{1Peter 3:18-20}.

- o Oh, My! Imagine the look on Satan's face when Jesus, The Victorious, walked in and began preaching! *"I AM THE RESURRECTION AND THE LIFE. WHOEVER BELIEVES IN ME, ALTHOUGH HE MAY DIE, YET HE SHALL LIVE"* [John 11:25].
    - • Imagine TRUTH reverberating through the caverns of hell!
- • He led captivity captive [Psalm 68:18-20; Ephesians 4:7-11].
    - o The Hebrew word for captivity (captives) in Strong's is #7628 which is from a word #7618 that means precious stone. It's equated to the stones in the breastplate of the High Priest and the flashes of light from them.
    - • He captured for Himself the precious stones, souls, the flashes of light that had been captured by satan even before the flood of Noah.
- • 1 Peter 3:18-20 tells us:
  For Christ the Messiah Himself, died for sins once for all, the Righteous for the unrighteous (the Just for the unjust, the Innocent for the guilty), that He might bring us to God. In His human body He was put to death but He was made alive in the Spirit in which He went and preached to the spirits in prison, (the souls of those who long before in the days of Noah had been disobedient, when God's patience waited during the building of the ark in which a few people, actually eight in number, were saved through water.
- • Then Psalm 68:18-20 tells us:

15

You have ascended on high, You have led captivity captive: You have received gifts for men; yes, [for] the rebellious also, that the LORD God might dwell [among them]. Blessed [be] the Lord, [who] daily loads us [with benefits, even] the God of our salvation. Selah. [He that is] our God [is] the God of salvation; and unto GOD the Lord [belong] the issues from death ^{KJV}.

Notice, the last sentence says that *"unto God the Lord belong the issues from death."* That word "Issues" is a Hebrew word, #8444 in the Strong's, and means "outgoing, border, a going out, extremity, end, source, escape." Death is not the end unless the Lord says it is! When our dreams die, they die in our image, constructed through our limited vision. We've done everything we can to make them happen, all to no avail. When they are resurrected, they are resurrected in the image of God as seen through His all knowing vision, reflecting His plan, His Kingdom, built on the sure foundation of His will for our lives.

I have seen many dreams die, perhaps even more in ministry than in the secular world. Some of the dreams I've seen die have been my own, many were dreams of others. Not everyone experiences the death of their dreams. Most of us do at one point or another. I recently heard that 85% of everyone who attends Bible School never preach one sermon. Perhaps that was not their goal. I've talked to many who have lived a life of struggle and disappointment because they thought their certification from an accredited Bible school would open doors—but didn't. A life in traditional ministry

16

is not an easy thing to lay hold of. However, if that is your call you will not be able to resist it and the Lord will strengthen you to be able to perform it.

Ministry has put on a new face today, the face of the market place. Not everyone is called to the pulpit or even para-church ministry. Know where your ministry is and do it. If you can be happy and successful doing anything else full-time and participating in traditional ministry part-time I suggest you not even consider full-time, traditional ministry. BUT, whatever your call is, if you are never satisfied unless you are "doing your dream," then I implore you, whatever it is:

NEVER GIVE UP!

However, if in "doing your dream" you seem to never reach a consistent level of success and even prosperity, it's time to look at a few things.

PREPARATION FOR RESURRECTION
1. I have a dream or dreams: (List the dream(s) you think or thought were lost.)
2. Hindrances in my life have been: (List hindrances of which you are aware whether real or perceived.)
3. Examine your heart. Is there hope in your heart?
4. Ask yourself, "What can I do to propagate hope turning it into faith?"
5. Prophetic words, words of confirmation I have received concerning my dream. (Use them as substance for faith. Use them to "war" for your appointed place.)
6. Count the costs.

7. Don't allow vital relationships to become bankrupt.
   - How can I invest in family?
   - How can I invest in friends?
   - How can I invest in mentors?
     o Who are my mentors?
   - How can I invest in protégés?
     o Who are my protégés?
8. Every day I will invest in my dream by:
9. What am I doing to keep my faith tank full?
10. How can I be more diligent about developing my dream, my business or ministry?
11. To whom am I accountable?
12. The foundation stones for my vision are:
13. My strategy for the future involves:
14. My progress markers (short term goals) are:
15. My long term goals include:

CHAPTER 2
GLORY CARRIERS

*"The glory on us demands that
God be glorified by our lives!"*

It's very important we recognize that we are carriers of the glory of God. I believe if we were truly conscious of that fact, it would affect every area of our lives. We would be more aware and alert to the effect of our actions and attitudes on others. I believe our conscience would be sharper and our character more sensitive to the leading of the Spirit. Look at The Prayer of the Bridegroom in John 17. I encourage you to become familiar with this entire chapter. It is life changing.

In verses 17-19 Jesus is asking the Father to sanctify His followers. Sanctify in this instance means to purify, consecrate, and separate, to make them holy ^{Strong's #37}. Then in verses 22-23 He says:

> *I have given to them the glory and honor which You have given Me, that they may be one (even) as We are one*: *I in them and You in Me, in order that they*

may become one and perfectly united, that the world may know and definitely recognize that you sent Me and that You have loved them (even) as You have loved Me.

One of the most telling and exciting verses in this chapter is verse 20. Jesus makes it clear that He's including me and you and everyone who will ever come to believe in Him. Here is what He says: *"Neither for these alone do I pray [it is not for their sake only that I make this request], but also for all those who will ever come to believe in (trust in, cling to, rely on) Me through their word and teaching."* He's talking about us! We believe because we have the testimony of the first followers, the disciples and apostles. He was looking into the future even to the end of time and including everyone up to the last person who will believe in Him even throughout the millennial reign.

So, we have been given "the glory." What we have to do is remember from Whom the glory actually comes and remember that the *magnificence, excellence, preeminence, dignity* and *grace* ^{Strong's #1391} are actually the extension of Christ in us. Only by His Spirit can we affect change and show forth the Kingdom of Heaven so that people are drawn to Him. If people are drawn to us and are not truly changed or come to a saving, life changing knowledge of Jesus Christ, we have failed.

We are carriers of the glory of God. But we are not to be lifted up (proud) or glorified (honored) for gifts and manifestations resulting from the indwelling Spirit of the living God. Our lives should bring honor to Jesus, the Son of God. To honor the Son honors the Father ^{John 5:23}. Bottom line, God gets all the credit. So, we should recognize that we are carriers of God's glory but never, never, never take credit for what He does through us.

Pride is an insidious beast. It often comes disguised in legalism and duty. When pride begins to feast on us we start thinking we're the only one who can do a certain thing or that at the very least no one can do it as well as we can. We often think that if we don't do it, it won't get done. Sometimes it shouldn't get done. If whatever we're doing "for Christ and the Kingdom of God" is being done through any motive other than love, we need to take a step back until love reigns and is evident in what we're doing [1 Corinthians 13:1-8, 13; Colossians 3:23].

The thing is, if we feel prideful or puffed up when we minister, or concerning our ministry and/or relationship with God, we're forgetting that it's only by His Spirit that these things are done. We begin taking the credit for what the Spirit is doing and thereby begin touching the glory God has put on us. We begin taking credit because of our education, "our" anointing, our popularity. We can go a long way on charisma, personality, knowledge of scripture, performance or even aggression. However, if it isn't the Spirit of God ministering through us, sooner or later we will fail and whatever we've done will not last.

In 2 Corinthians 12:9, the Lord told Paul that His strength and power are made perfect and show themselves most effective in our weakness. So Paul states that he would rather "take pleasure" in his weaknesses so the power of Christ might rest upon him.

In Colossians 3:22-24, Paul tells us that whatever we say or do should be done as though for the Lord and accomplished in such a way that shows our dependence upon

Him, giving glory and praise to God the Father through the Son.

Jesus tells us in John 15:4-5 that we should live in Him, and He will live in us. We cannot produce good works or "fruit" unless we live in Him any more than a branch from a vine can bear grapes once it is detached from the vine. It's only in Him, by Him and through Him we live and move and have our existence ^{Acts 17:28}.

- It isn't our education.
- Our anointing.
- Our personality.
- Our ministry.
- It isn't even our life.
  - **IT'S ALL ABOUT HIM.**

Interestingly—for Him—it's all about us.
- He came to earth for us ^{Isaiah 9:6-7; John 1:10-13; 3:16-17}.
- He was born as the son of man for us ^{Matthew 1:23; Luke 9:22-26; John 3:16-17; (The books of Matthew, Mark, Luke, and John}.
- He lived a sinless life under the law for us ^{2 Corinthians 5:21; Hebrews 4:15}.
- He surrendered His will for us ^{Matthew 26:39, 42, 44; Mark 14:34-39; Luke 22:42-44; John 6:38}.
- He bore our grief and our sorrows ^{Isaiah 53:4}.
- He took our shame ^{Isaiah 50:6; Hebrews 12:2}.
- He carried our guilt as His own ^{2 Corinthians 5:21}.
- He bore our sins: ^{1 Peter 2:24}.
- He bore our sickness and disease ^{Isaiah 53:4; Matthew 8:16-17}.
- He allowed Himself to be beaten near death with a whip that stripped out chunks of flesh—for us (for

our healing) Matthew 27:26; Mark 15:15; John 19:1; 1 Peter 2:24; Isaiah 53:5.

- He became cursed on the cross for us Galatians 3:13.
- He became sin for us 2 Corinthians 5:21.
- He was despised and rejected for us Matthew 21:42; 27:17-21; Mark 12:10, 15:11-13; Luke 10:17, 23:18-23.
- He was wrongly accused for us Matthew 27:4; Mark 14-15; Luke 23.
- He was smitten of God for us, forsaken by the Father because of us Isaiah 53:4; Matthew 27:46; Mark 15:34.
- He was wounded for our rebellion (transgressions) Isaiah 53:5.
- He was bruised for our perversity, depravity (iniquity) Isaiah 53:5.
- He was a casualty of capital punishment for us Matthew 27:17-21; Mark 14:11-13; Luke 23:18-23; John 11:50;18:14,38-40; 19:4, 6.
- He gave His life, willingly laid down His life for us John 10:14-18; 15:13;.
- He rose from the dead for us Romans 8:29; Revelation 1:5.
- He gave us His righteousness Romans 3:22; 1 Corinthians 1:30.
- He gave us His victory over death and the grave 1 Corinthians 15:53-57.
- He gave us His Glory John 17:22.
- He gave us authority over all the power of the enemy Luke 10:19.
- He gave us all we need to partake of His divine nature 2 Peter 1:3-4.
- He gave us eternal life John 2:25, 5:11-13, 20 3:14-17, 10:28-29, 17:1-3; Romans 5:12, 6:23.

o How can we not love Him when He so loved us and gave Himself for us ^{Galatians 1:4; Titus 2:13-14; 1 John 4:15-19}?

Does He expect anything from us for these wondrous gifts? Certainly! In Luke 14, verse 26, He tells us that if we don't hate everything in our lives, our families, even our own life in comparison to how we love Him, we can't even be His followers. We must be willing to violently overthrow the things of this world to gain the Kingdom of Heaven ^{Matthew 11:12}.

EVEN SO! We need to come into agreement with Him concerning who and what He says we are.

- We are:
    o The Light of the World ^{Matthew 5:14}.
    o The Salt of the Earth ^{Matthew 5:13}.
    o The Hands of Christ ^{Acts 4:29-30}.
    o Anointed ^{2 Corinthians 1:21-22}.
    o Appointed ^{Luke 10:1}.
    o Heirs of God. Joint Heirs with Christ ^{Romans 8:17}.
    o Called ^{Matthew 20:16; 1 Peter 2:9; Revelation 17:14}.
    o Chosen ^{Matthew 20:16; 1 Peter 2:9; Revelation 17:14}.
    o His Body ^{Romans 12:5; 1 Corinthians 12:27, 12:12-20, 27; Ephesians 4:4-6}.
    o Sealed ^{2 Corinthians 1:22; Ephesians 1:13, 4:30}.

Now, I know there are a number of things we could add to this list, but here, we'll look only at those listed above. The items on this list will demonstrate some of the aspects of living in His glory.

- If we are "the light of the world," we should be examples of life lived in the light of Truth ^{Ephesians 5:8-10}.

- If we are "the salt of the earth" we should make a difference in the "flavor" of life, our own as well as the lives of those around us. We should also be involved in stopping corruption by exercising righteous living standards and letting our voice be heard in government Colossians 4:5-6; Mark 9:50.

- If we are "The Hands of Christ," we should be reaching out to help the poor, doing good works and healing all who come to us Matthew 10:7-8; Luke 10:9; Mark 16:17-18; Acts 4:29-30.

- If we are "Anointed," the gifts and fruit of Holy Spirit should be evident in our lives Acts 10:38; 2 Corinthians 1:21; Galatians 5:22-25; Ephesians 5:9; 1 Corinthians 12:4-13.

- If we are "Appointed," we should have a clear direction, a goal, a vision, focused upon the God given plan for our lives Luke 10:1-11; Acts 22:10; 2 Timothy 1:11.

- If we are "Heirs of God—Joint Heirs with Christ," we should demonstrate a close relationship with God, walking in the authority and the integrity of our Father's house, in the confidence of His provision, protection and leadership Romans 8:14-17; Galatians 3:26-29, 4:4-7; Ephesians 1:10-14; Titus 3:4-7.

- If we are "Called," we should understand the honor of His invitation and learn the protocol of His Kingdom— walking as sons and daughters of God for we are His offspring Romans 6:4; Colossians 2:6-7; 1 John 2:6; Acts 17:28; Ephesians 1:10-14.

- If we are "Chosen," we should abandon things that do not reflect our destination, pressing toward the mark for the

prize of the high calling of God in Christ Jesus ^{John 14:16, 19;}
Ephesians 1:3-6; Philippians 3:14; 1 Peter 2:1-9

- If we are "His Body" we should live as if we are all joined together in one body, not only are we one in His body, we should live as if we are members (part) of one another, for indeed we are ^{Romans 12:1-2, 5; 1 Corinthians 6:19-20;} 12:12-27; Ephesians 5:30

- If we are "Sealed," we should live as one betrothed, set aside for His purposes causing no offense to Holy Spirit by whom we are sealed ^{2 Corinthians 1:21-22; Ephesians 1:13, 4:30; 1} Corinthians 6:11; 2 Corinthians 11:2

This glory He has given us is dependent upon relationship with Him. As a matter of fact, everything about the Christian walk is about relationship; relationship with Jesus, relationship with Holy Spirit, relationship with our Father, and relationship with one another.

We actually see this in Jesus' own ministry. Everything He did was to bring glory to God, to glorify the Father, and everything was done through and by relationship. In John 5, verse 30, Jesus shows His total dependence, the leaning of His entire personality on and His trust in the Father.

I am able to do nothing from Myself (independently, of My own accord—but only as I am taught by God and as I get His orders). Even as I hear, I judge (I decide as I am bidden to decide. As the voice comes to Me so I give a decision) and My judgment is right (just, righteous), because I do not seek or consult My own will [I have no desire to do what is pleasing to

Myself, My own aim, My own purpose] but only the will and pleasure of the Father Who sent Me ^{John 5:30}.

As we read through the New Testament we find a great deal of emphasis on the importance of glorifying both the Father and the Son, Jesus. Actually the entire Bible emphasizes the need for a strong, deep relationship with the triune God.

Let's talk about what is often called our "horizontal" relationships—relationship with our fellows. There's no room for jealousy. We may call it a "spirit of competition." No matter what you call it, it is jealousy. It springs from a feeling of inadequacy, though pride often hides the true identity of this monstrous manifestation. We feel threatened in one way or another and because of that feeling, we become instruments of division in the Body of Christ.

... love is as strong as death, jealousy is as hard and cruel as Sheol (the place of the dead). Its flashes of fire a most vehement flame (the very flame of the Lord) ^{Song of Solomon 8:6}!

If we love one another, as members or part of ourselves, we are not going to be jealous of anyone's successes. Rather we will help them any way we can and rejoice in their success and advancement. Also, we will do whatever we can to walk in excellency so that our life enhances the lives of those with whom we are one.

If we remain vitally united to Him and His words live, are active and productive in us, whatever we ask will be done for us. This shows relationship, His "sap" running through our veins, bearing the fruit of relationship. This is fruit that glorifies and honors God. Our Lord, Jesus, loves us just like the Father loves Him. If we keep His commandments we will live in His love. His commandment is that we love one another even as He loves us [John 15:1-12].

We'll look a little further at love in a later chapter.

PREPARATION FOR RESURRECTION

1. My self-image can best be described as:
2. Can I envision the above person as a repository of God's glory?
   - Why or why not?
3. How does what I do or want to do bring glory to God?
4. How am I allowing Holy Spirit to guide me right now?
5. How can I cooperate more fully with Holy Spirit?
6. How can I be used to dispel darkness?
7. How does my life flavor my area of influence?
8. In what areas and lives do I have influence?
9. How can I be used to stop corruption in these areas and/or lives?
10. How can I expand my areas of influence?
11. Do I see myself as God sees me?
    - If not, what prevents me?

CHAPTER 3
IT'S UP TO YOU

"A simple change in attitude can change the heart.
A change of heart
Will change our actions and the outcome of our lives."

Sometimes it's difficult to look honestly at our self and choose to not only recognize but also deal with character issues. It's also often difficult to let go of bad habits and even more difficult to leave life-long acquaintances who are contaminating or corrupting influence in our life. However, this is exactly what we are instructed to do in 2 Timothy 2. Let's take a look at verses 20 and 21:

But in a great house there are not only vessels of gold and silver, but also utensils of wood and earthenware, and some for honorable and noble use and some for menial and ignoble use. ***So whoever cleanses himself from what is ignoble and unclean, who separates himself from contact with contaminating and corrupting influences,*** *will then himself be a vessel set apart and useful for honorable and noble* *purposes, consecrated and profitable to the Master, fit and ready for any good work.*

You see what it says here? Even if a person were made for dishonorable, ignoble or unclean purposes, they can cleanse themselves of these things and become a vessel of honor. That person can become consecrated and profitable to the Master, fit and ready for any good work. We don't have to stay the way we've always been. We truly can change. The next verse has another clue to cleansing ourselves:

Shun youthful lusts and flee from them, and aim at and pursue righteousness (all that is virtuous and good, right living, conformity to the will of God in thought, word, and deed); and aim at and pursue faith, love, and peace (harmony and concord with others) in fellowship with all Christians who call upon the Lord out of a pure heart [2 Timothy 2:22].

We'll discuss this in more detail later. Long story short, don't remain the way you've always been [1 Corinthians 13:11]! When we refuse to change we become like stagnant water—like Lazarus. Life begins to deteriorate. The reason the Dead Sea in Israel is called the Dead Sea is because there is no life in it. Water flows in but there is no out-flow. Not only is there no life in the water except for a few micro-organisms, there is no life around the Dead Sea on land. We become like that. Not only do we not experience growth, we tend at least to attempt to hold our loved ones and friends in that place of death. We resent it when they insist on growing, being different or even more when they try to change us. That's a trap we need to avoid, even at great cost. A strong warning is found in 2 Timothy 3:6-7 where we are told we can be easily led astray because we are ever learning but never coming to a knowledge of truth.

(<u>Preparation for Resurrection</u> will be divided throughout this chapter due to its length and the various aspects of self examination covered.)
PREPARATION FOR RESURRECTION

1. Do I actually believe I can be a vessel fit for the Master's use?
2. What wood and clay do I need to purge from myself?
   - How can I cooperate with Holy Spirit to purge myself of these?
3. In what ways am I already fit for the Master's use?
4. I see gold shining through the clay because I……
5. If you cannot see gold in yourself, ask someone you really trust to be honest with you to help you see your gold.

SOME STEPS WE MAY NEED TO TAKE

Throughout this book we will be carefully examining ourselves. The keys to success are within our heart and in our relationships, especially our relationship with God. In forthcoming chapters, we will examine various influences over which we have control. We'll also look at some things over which we do not have control. Let's begin with a quick overview of how to take the first steps toward attaining our dreams or promises.

Guard Your Heart

The Word of God tells us in Proverbs 4:23 that we should guard our heart, our inner man, more strictly than we guard anything else.

Keep and guard your heart with all vigilance and above all that you guard, for out of it flow the issues (springs) of life.

According to Strong's #3820, our heart is our mind, will, understanding and the seat of our emotions, passions, appetites and courage. It's where our determination, inclinations, resolution, and conscience are stored.

Look at and consider these definitions of "heart" carefully. When something weird or wonderful comes out of our mouth, we don't have to wonder where it came from. It comes from our heart. The same is true with outbursts of anger or overwhelming love. It comes from our heart.

Please understand how important it is to guard your heart. If it has been unguarded at any time and then not carefully examined and purged, it can corrupt everything you do, everything you say, everything you feel—perhaps most importantly—how you understand.

Now, what are the "issues (springs)" of life as stated in the above verse? Strong's #8444 shows that the issues or springs of life are the outgoing, border, extremity, end, source, and/or escape. It further amplifies this meaning as source of life and escape from death. So, this obscure little verse is full of mystery. It is to our benefit to come to an understanding of these mysteries not leaving anything in our heart unexamined, whether things leading to life, or things leading to death.

In Psalm 119:11 we are told that we can keep guard on our inner being by storing up God's Word in our heart so we don't sin. In Psalm 139, David asks help from the Lord to keep his heart:

"Search me thoroughly, O God, and know my heart!
Try me and know my thoughts! And see if there is any
wicked or hurtful way in me, and lead me in the way
everlasting" [v.23-24].

We don't have to do this alone. We only need to trust/rely on the Lord, leaning our whole personality, all our understanding on Him [Proverbs 3:5-6]. Holy Spirit will lead us in guarding and cleansing our heart.

We're all familiar with the account of the wealthy man in Matthew 19 who wanted to know what *"good thing he should do that he might have eternal life."* When Jesus told him to sell everything and give the proceeds to the poor then follow Him, the man was unable to do that. His possessions possessed his heart. He had come asking how to attain eternal life and when given the answer he exhibited the same spirit that Esau operated in. Esau sold his inheritance for a bowl of soup. This man sold eternal life for earthly possessions. He knew scripture and had kept all the law all his life. BUT! What he knew and what he sought of Jesus were not his treasure. Eternal life was not as valuable to him as what he had on earth. His possessions were his treasure.

Let's look at some scriptures that define heart treasure and the outflow of it. In Matthew 6:21 we are reminded that where our treasure is, that's where our heart will be found. This scripture speaks of treasure that can be stored up, things that have a value attached. Our heart is attached to what we value. Truly valuable things cannot be stolen from us. They have a connection to the eternal realm of heaven. When our focus is on earthly treasure we are unable to accurately value the true treasures of eternity.

In Matthew 12, verses 34-37, we discover that our heart is like a storehouse. What we speak comes from the overflow of our heart. The Lord also makes it clear that on judgment day we will be either condemned and sentenced or we will be acquitted by those words. Interestingly here, the Lord is showing us that we distribute what's in our heart whether good or bad. *From the overflow of the heart the mouth speaks* ^{Matthew 12:34; Luke 6:45}. We need to be sure that the treasure that's laid up in our hearts is of the sort that will do good and not harm.

*The good man **from his inner good treasure flings forth good things**, and the evil man out of his inner evil storehouse flings forth evil* ^{Matthew 12:35; Luke 6:45}.

Luke 6:43-44 and Matthew 12:33 tell us that a bad, rotten tree cannot bear good fruit. Neither can a good tree bear rotten fruit. Picture words as seeds of what's in your own heart. Every time we speak, we are planting seeds.

Proverbs 26:22 tells us that if we are *a whisperer or slanderer our words are like dainty morsels or words of sport to some, but to others are like deadly wounds; and they go down into the innermost parts of the body or of the victim's nature.* We need to count the cost of the harvest of our words. What will our harvest of words look like? When they find soil in the hearts of those to whom we speak will our word seeds bring forth life or will they cause deadly wounds?

Are we liberally flinging out seeds of love and healing, peace and joy, wisdom, knowledge and understanding? Or, are we "flinging" seeds of bitterness and strife, heart weeds that will have to be pulled out of the hearts of the hearers? We need to keep close check on our heart—our storehouse of seed—so the overflow brings life.

I've seen and known people who believe they are good and that they wouldn't hurt anyone purposely. But they are so full of pain, disappointment, and hatred that even the good they aim for is tainted with bitterness and pain. I have been such a person.

On the other hand, I know very good people who sometimes get wounded or angry and intend to strike back. But when they open their mouth mercy pours forth and both they and the person who hurt them are healed. The overflow of their heart is goodness and kindness. A good tree cannot bear rotten fruit.

Our actions, our thoughts, and our words take their cue from what's in our hearts. With His Word hidden in our hearts, our actions will be stimulated by what is right. If we can't locate what we need in the treasures of our heart, we must seek it out in the treasure house of His Word. We seek council from those who we trust to know and understand God's Word. We turn to the Word of God to find out what we should do in every circumstance or situation. Mark 4:22

tells us that things are hidden temporarily only as a means to revelation. As we search it out, we gain treasure in our heart and that treasure will remain for us to use over and over again.

If we are accustomed to watching secular television, reading horoscopes or consulting psychics, that's what will come out of our mouth. Something about those things can cause us to think we have superior knowledge. We become prideful which births jealousies and strife in our hearts. The Word of God tells us that *such wisdom is earthly, unspiritual, animal, even devilish or demoniacal* [James 3:15]. This is not acceptable in the life of a Christian. *But wisdom from above is first of all pure (undefiled): then it is peace loving, courteous (considerate and gently)* [James 3:17]. God is well able to instruct us. He is omnipresent, present everywhere at all times [Matthew 28:20]. He is omniscient, knowing everything, the only wise God [Proverbs 2:4-5; Isaiah 40:9-10; Romans 16:27; I Timothy 1:17; Jude 1:25]. He is omnipotent, all powerful [Revelation 19:6]. He is trustworthy and faithful.

PREPARATION FOR RESURRECTION

6. The treasures of my heart are:
   - I value them because……
   - They are valuable to the Kingdom of God because……
7. What standard do I use to place value on the things of my heart?
8. Do the things I value change depending on who I'm with and what I'm doing?
9. What do I need to do to guard my heart more carefully?

Guard Your Thoughts

The first time the word "thought" appears in the Bible, it is a Hebrew word, #559 in Strong's and means: to say, to answer, to say in one's heart. Other words translated "thought" also mean to intercede, to promise, sing, resemble, to fear or be anxious, eye and many other things. The Greek meanings are complimentary to these.

Thoughts are very powerful. Thoughts are actually words to the Lord. He knows our thoughts from a distance, even before we think them ^{Psalm 139:2}. Several places in the gospels, we read that Jesus knew their thoughts. Knowing, perceiving, He responded what they were thinking or what they really wanted to know rather than what they asked ^{Matthew 9:4, 12:25; Luke 5:22, 6:8, 11:17}.

Even more astounding to me is it was the thoughts of man that caused God to regret He had even made mankind. We are told in Genesis 6:5-6:

*The Lord saw that the wickedness of man was great in the earth, and that **every imagination and intention of all human thinking was only evil continually.** And the Lord regretted that He had made man on the earth, and He was grieved at heart.*

Oh My! We all want to please God but how many of us consider that our thoughts may be offensive to God? It just could be that when we consider the most important thing to change about ourselves, we should consider our thoughts. Here's an example of how important thoughts are:

In Proverbs 23:6-8, we are being cautioned to beware of those who have *a hard, grudging, and envious eye* and who think perversely. Even if they offer food or anything else, they don't really mean it because as they think in their heart, so are they. They think grudgingly so will begrudge what you eat or what you take even though they offer it to you. So, basically they think "cursingly," resentfully toward you.

The same principle applies to a good man. A good person is blessed when you are able to receive what is offered. Good people think differently than the wicked. Giving is an extension of who they are so they are improved when you receive. The thoughts of their heart are to bless not curse.

Our thoughts are seeds for action. Jeremiah 6:19 tells us that God will give us the *fruit of our thoughts.* There have been times I have prayed for crop failure. When we permit our thoughts to wander, all too often unchecked thoughts lead to lust and other ungodly pursuits. These thoughts often turn into obsession and soon override everything we know is right and proper—good. We are told in James 1:14-15:

Every person is tempted when he is drawn away, enticed and baited by his own evil desire (lust, passions). Then the evil desire (thought), when it has conceived, gives birth to sin and sin when it is fully matured, brings forth death.

WOW!!! The thought gives birth to sin, opening the door to death! So—the conception of an evil thought can be the seed of death!

We never "accidentally" do anything. First, we think of it, then, if we ponder it—or think of it often—we do it. Left unchecked, this process recurs until we've done something so many times that it becomes a habit, second nature to us. When we recognize that what we're thinking is not right, we have the opportunity to avoid problems and even to avoid developing negative character issues. *"As he thinks, so is he"* proverbs 3:7.

We are even encouraged to repent so that perhaps *the thought of our heart may be forgiven us* ^{Acts 8:22}. The Lord tells us that to lust (think with passion) about something is the same as doing it. The specific scripture in Matthew 5 pertains to lusting after a woman, but the principle is the same for anything. When we lust, apply our thoughts passionately to fleshly things, we have set up an idol and abandoned our focus on God.

As we mature, our thought processes should change. Paul puts it this way in 1 Corinthians 13:11:

*When I was a child, I talked like a child, **I thought like a child, I reasoned like a child; now that I have become a man, I am done with childish ways and have put them aside.***

We have to learn to think responsibly. The Lord knows our thoughts before we even think them. *The Lord searches all hearts and understands the imaginations (form, purpose, framework) the wanderings of the thoughts* ^{1 Chronicles 28:9}. King David encouraged that search:

Search me (thoroughly), O God, and know my heart!
***Try me and know my thoughts** see if there is any*

wicked or hurtful way in me, and lead me in the way everlasting ^{Psalm 139:23-24}!

*Let the words of my mouth and **the meditations of my heart** be acceptable in your sight O Lord* ^{Psalm 19:14}.

Proverbs 16:3 tells us that if we commit our works to the Lord and trust Him completely, He will cause our thoughts to become agreeable to His will and our plans shall be established and succeed.

In Proverbs 21:5 we are told that the thoughts of the diligent tend only to plenteousness. Here's a key. Be diligent to know the status of your business/ministry and your thoughts will lead to plenteousness ^{Proverbs 22:29; Proverbs 27:23}.

Jeremiah 6:19 tells us that the Lord brings the fruit of our thoughts upon us. Also, in Matthew 15:18-20 and Mark 7:20-23, Jesus tells us that it's our evil thoughts and desires that defile.

Medical research has proven that most chronic diseases are caused by emotions, mental stress, and unforgiveness. We develop psycho-somatic symptoms. Psycho-somatic symptoms are physical manifestations of our inability or refusal to cope with life as we perceive it. In other words they are the result of our thought processes. Even when developed from psycho-somatic symptoms, these diseases can actually kill us because the diseases and their effects on our bodies are real regardless of their cause. There are cases reported in medical research articles of patients with terminal diseases who were cured after they forgave or let go of bitterness. ^(Britannica Concise Dictionary, Wikipedia, and various medical research sites and schools)

I know sometimes it is very difficult to change the way we think. However, we can always find help in scripture. One scripture that helped me overcome difficult thought patterns was 2 Corinthians 10:3-5:

*For though we walk (live) in the flesh, we are not carrying on our warfare according to the flesh and using mere human weapons. For the weapons of our warfare are not physical (weapons of flesh and blood), but they are mighty before God for the overthrow and destruction of strongholds, inasmuch as we refute arguments and theories and reasonings and every proud and lofty thing that sets itself up against the true knowledge of God; **and we lead every thought and purpose away captive into the obedience of Christ**.*

How do we do that? Glad you asked. We can choose our thoughts—what we think about and how we think it. When we find ourselves entertaining negative, perverse, or fantasy thoughts, we repent, ask forgiveness, then replace those thoughts with positive, life giving thoughts. We use the Word of God. Make it a part of your daily routine, give it priority.

His Word should be the way we start every day. It's much more effective than coffee and goes a lot further toward making your day successful. Crave it as you crave your favorite food. Fall in love with the Word of God. Meditate on it every chance you get. At stoplights, in traffic jams, instead of thinking about the delay, think about a scripture or pray in the Spirit. I know, that's an easy one, everyone knows to do that. Right? Well, let's look at some other applications.

When someone wants to argue, think about scripture. When someone offends you, pray for them and for yourself. After all, the Lord said that offenses would come "*but woe to the man by whom they come*" ^{Matthew18:7; Luke 17:1}. They need prayer. Pray for mercy! Pray for yourself so you do not take offense. Notice the phrase is to "take offense." If our heart is full of God's word and our mind is centered on Him, we are much less likely to take offense, to become offended.

The more we consider the Word of God the more clearly we hear His voice and the less we question, "Was that me or was it the Lord?" We learn to know His voice by knowing His Word. He will never contradict His Word so if we know His character revealed through knowing His Word we will clearly hear and understand His direction and guidance. This is the first step toward becoming more like Him.

For the Word that God speaks is alive and full of power (making it active, operative, energizing, and effective); it is sharper than any two-edged sword, penetrating to the dividing line of the breath of life (soul) and the immortal spirit, and of joints and marrow (of the deepest parts of our nature) **exposing and sifting and analyzing and judging the very thoughts and purposes of the heart** ^{Hebrews 4:12}.

Wow! The Word of God exposes, sifts, analyzes, and judges the thoughts and purposes of the heart!

Guarding your thoughts and grounding them on the Word of God will cause your words to carry the weight and authority backed up by heaven.

PREPARATION FOR RESURRECTION

10. Am I conscious of the fact that imagination was given to mankind as a way to communicate with God?
11. Am I comfortable knowing God hears my thoughts?
12. Do I use my imagination to entertain vain, empty, powerless thoughts?
13. How can I change my thinking—guarding my thoughts?
14. What do I most often meditate on?
15. What scriptures can I incorporate into my meditations to begin building a more godly thought process?
16. What habitual thought patterns do I use that shut out light and life?
17. Do I have good thought patterns I can build on to cause more
change in my inner man—pushing darkness out of my soul?

Guard Your Mouth

We've already learned that the mouth speaks from the overflow of the heart. Let's examine the power of our words. Life and death, blessing and cursing, love and hate, all come through our mouth.

Death and life are in the power of the tongue, and they who indulge in it shall eat the fruit of it (for death or life) ^{Proverbs 18:21}.

We really need to fill our heart with wisdom, knowledge and understanding of this scripture so that when our heart overflows into our mouth it brings life, not death, to ourselves and/or to others. Perhaps we should pray daily Psalm 141, verses 3 and 4:

Set a guard, O Lord, before my mouth; *keep watch at the door of my lips. Incline my heart not to submit to any evil thing or to be occupied in deeds of wickedness with men who work iniquity; and let me not eat of their dainties.*

And—Look at this:
But the human tongue can be tamed by no man. It is a restless (undisciplined, irreconcilable) evil, full of deadly poison. *With it we bless the Lord and Father, and with it we curse men who were made in God's likeness! Out of the same mouth come forth blessing and cursing.* **These things, my brethren, ought not to be so** ^{James 3:8-10}.

44

Another scripture tells us we lie if we say we love the Father but hate our brother [1 John 4:20]. If we love one another, we are not going to curse each other. We are going to speak life, blessing, and prosperity from the overflow of our hearts. We need to cooperate with the Lord so that the words of our mouth and the meditation of our heart is acceptable in His sight [Psalm 19:14]. Then, since our heart is filled with things acceptable to the Lord, no foul or polluting language, nor evil word or unwholesome or worthless talk will come out of our mouth. We will only speak what is good and beneficial to the spiritual progress of ourselves and others as is fitting to the need and the occasion that it may be a blessing and give grace to those who hear it [Ephesians 4:29].

Ecclesiastes 5, verse 6 tells us to not let our mouth cause our flesh/body to sin. Proverbs 10:11 says *the mouth of the uncompromisingly righteous man is a well of life but the mouth of the wicked conceals violence.*

WE MUST GUARD OUR MOUTH.

PREPARATION FOR RESURRECTION

18. What kind of seeds am I planting with my mouth and actions?
    - Do I encourage or participate in gossip?
    - Am I a back-stabber?
    - Do I "vent" poisonous words about others?
    - Do I "vent" destructive, angry, judgmental, or slanderous words to others?
    - Do I exhort, encourage, honor others with my words?
19. How do I or how can I challenge others to measure their words for good.

20. Do I have things I habitually say that hurt my future, my life,
    my relationships?
21. Have I asked the Lord to set a guard on my mouth to prevent my sinning against Him?

Guard Your Eyes:

It has been said that the eyes are the window of the soul. This has certainly proven to be true in several aspects of understanding. Our eyes also reveal physical problems. Many doctors first check our eyes when we're ill. The eyes will show what's going on in our body, if our organs are working right, if we are taking drugs. They will show if we have had a broken bone. By looking at our eyes many people can tell if we are in pain, physical or emotional. They are seeing into us. I've heard the word "intimacy" transposed to "into-me-see." The more closely we are involved with others, the more likely we will be able to see past words to the emotion or thought behind the words. Our understanding of such things and interpretation of what we see depends a great deal how much treasure of God's Word is hidden in our hearts—how we think.

The Word of God has a lot to say about the eyes. Let's look at some of the supporting scriptures.

- Winking Eye

    *A **worthless person, a wicked man**, is he who goes about with a perverse (contrary, wayward) mouth.*
    ***He winks with his eyes**, he speaks by shuffling or tapping with his feet, he makes signs (to mislead and deceive) and teaches with his fingers* ^{Proverbs 6:12-13}.
    *He who **winks** with the eye **(craftily and with malice)** causes sorrow...* ^{Proverbs 10:10}.

I have seen the wink used to convey several different messages. I've seen it mean, "Shhhh. Don't tell anyone." I've seen it mean, "You're cute! I'm interested!" Sometimes it conveys agreement. Sometimes it means, "I'll get you for that!" Acts 17:30 tells us that there was a time when God "winked" at ignorance *"but now commands all men everywhere to repent"* ᴷᴶⱽ. The Amplified puts it this way:

> *Such former ages of ignorance God,* **it is true, ignored (winked) and allowed to pass unnoticed;** *but now He charges all people everywhere to repent (to change their minds for the better and heartily to amend their ways, with abhorrence of their past sins).*

A wink is never—nothing. There is always a message conveyed with a wink.

- Single Eye (Full of Light)
  To have "a single eye" means that we choose to see the goodness of God. There are two sets of eyes, the natural eye and the spiritual eye sometimes referred to as our conscience. If our conscience is clear, light (righteousness) will flood our being. Eye as used in Luke 11:34 is Strong's Greek #3788 and means the eyes of the mind, the faculty of knowing. Let's look at that scripture understanding the eye as the faculty of knowing.

> *Your eye (*faculty of knowing*) is the lamp of your body; when your eye (your conscience) (*your faculty of knowing*) is sound and fulfilling its office, your whole body is full of light; but when it is not sound and is not fulfilling its office, your body is full of darkness. Be careful, therefore, that the light that is in you is not darkness* [Luke 11:34-36; Matthew 6:22-23].

So, when our conscience, inner eye, our faculty of knowing, is not working right we cannot discern good and evil. We can become full of darkness because there is no "stop-check," no understanding upon which to base discernment and make proper decisions.

Let's look briefly at a few other scriptures. Have you noticed when someone says, "Let me think," the first thing most people do is close their eyes? Sometimes that's to be able to focus, but look at this:

He who shuts his eyes to devise perverse things and who compresses his lips (as if in concealment) brings evil to pass Proverbs 16:30.

This is a person who devises secret plans, normally based on conjecture. "What if . . .?" Or, "Now, when I do this, they'll do that." "If I say this, they'll say that." He sets ambushments so he can be in control and to "have his way." On the other hand, there is another type person who shuts their eyes.

Now these scriptures, Isaiah 33:15, are the response to verse 14 that asks the question "Who can survive the judgments of the Lord." The answer is:

*He who walks righteously and speaks uprightly, who despises gain from fraud and from oppression, who shakes his hand free from the taking of bribes, **who stops his ears from hearing of bloodshed and shuts his eyes to avoid looking upon evil.***

WOW! How clear is that? How simple is that? In the current American culture, we are fascinated with evil. Just imagine if all the movies and television shows we watched demonstrated goodness, kindness, peace and joy. Suppose we saw people helping one another and living in harmony.

- Would we then tolerate the violence that surrounds us today?
- Would there even be the extent of violence to be tolerated?
- Is it possible that people would be acting out what they saw, the harmony, the kindness, the goodness they witnessed with their eyes as many are today acting out the disharmony?
- If the news media reported the good things that are happening around the country at least as often as they report the bad, would we be encouraged rather than alarmed?
- How would it affect us if we stop our ears from hearing of bloodshed and shut our eyes to avoid looking upon evil?

With our eyes, we feed our soul. What we read, watch, look at, is imprinted on our minds and often, as if with indelible ink. If we add any other of our sensory receptors, touch, hearing, smell or taste, the effect of what we have seen is multiplied. Then if our life forces are stimulated by that sight and our participation with it, it becomes even more deeply implanted in our mind's eye so that we often experience the "sight" when we remember what we saw.

- This can stimulate terror or anger if we have witnessed violence.
- It can stimulate us sexually if we have looked at pornography.

- It can stimulate love as we remember our children in our arms, their little faces looking up at us full of trust.

Here are a couple more significant scriptures:

I dictated a covenant (an agreement) to my eyes; how then could I look lustfully upon a girl [Job 31:1]. (Or anyone or anything? Author's note.)
I will set no base or wicked thing before my eyes. I hate the work of them that turn aside from the right path; it shall not grasp hold of me [Psalm 101:3].

Have you considered making a covenant with your eyes to guard them from things that pollute your entire being? When we allow our eyes to look at ungodly things we actually cloud the thoughts, intents and purposes of our heart. In the beginning, it's like a watermark on paper. We don't notice it when it's covered with writing or graphics but it's still there. A trained eye can actually see how it affects the quality of the ink or toner used to print over it. Watermarks are used to mark our money so that it can't be counterfeited unless someone has the watermarked paper. Watermarks can be contrasted to become almost invisible or to be prominent. As we repeatedly expose our eyes to ungodliness, that mark on our heart becomes more prominent and soon becomes a guide to where we're going rather than just an indication of where we've been.

In the same way, habitually looking on godly things will guide us toward holy living, marking our hearts with righteousness, peace and joy.

WE MUST GUARD OUR EYES

The light in the eyes of him whose heart is joyful rejoices the heart of others. . . [Proverbs 15:30].

Some people can speak very clearly with their eyes. I know a woman who could cause dogs to cringe just by the way she looked at them. On the other hand, I know people who can call those same dogs with eyes of love and they feel invited to come for a pat. Men know when a woman is available simply by the way she looks at them. They can tell if she's "all out available," if she's available to "the right person" or if she is "completely unavailable" or off the market—not available at all. Eyes are used to entice, warn, direct, encourage and acknowledge. Eyes can make people stop in their tracks, approach—carefully or enthusiastically, sit down, shut up, speak up, or get out. Eyes reveal confidence, understanding, insecurity, doubt, distrust, questions, anger, hurt, joy, and love as well as many other things.

Eyes often speak louder than words. My mom trained us, her children, to obey her eyes. When we were in public, she didn't have to say anything with her voice or even snap her fingers. She could look at us then at her feet and we knew we were to sit down and be quiet.

**One of my favorite memories of my Mom is of her dancing eyes,
full of joy, mischief and love.**

WHAT ARE YOUR EYES SEEING?
WHAT ARE YOUR EYES SAYING?

PREPARATION FOR RESURRECTION

22. What am I looking at that creates problems for me? (TV, magazines, books, movies, etc.)
23. What do my eyes say about me?
    - Ask your friends what they see your eyes say.
24. Do I use my eyes to influence other people?
    - Do I flirt?
    - Warn?
    - Persuade?
    - Insult?
    - Encourage?
    - Sympathize?
    - Challenge?
    - Lie?
        - What are my eyes saying?

Guard Your Ears

We all know to not listen to vulgarity, profanity and such, although, sometimes, it is impossible to avoid. Any time we are in public places we are exposed to all manner of ear-pollution. It's a good plan to take the time every morning to ask the Lord to set a guard on our minds so such doesn't penetrate our heart. It also doesn't hurt to pray every evening (and periodically through the day) that we be cleansed from ear-pollution. However, profanity and vulgarity are not the only ear-polluters. Gossip is treacherous.

Guarding our ears is not just being careful about what we listen to. It's also about how we listen. The following scripture has been much misunderstood. Many people consider it to be connected with giving and receiving materially. It's actually connected with hearing and applying what we hear. The Amplified is very clear on this.

And He said to them, "Be careful what you are hearing. The measure of thought and study you give to the truth you hear will be the measure of virtue and knowledge that comes back to you and more besides will be given to you who hear Mark 4:24.

Now, this is also true if we allow our mind to dwell on profanities, vulgarities, lies, confusion, gossip and such that bombard our ears every day. If we think on those things that cause disunity, there will be disunity and we are very likely to be the source of it. If we consider the dirty joke we heard "at the water cooler" or any other place, our mind will begin picturing the things of that joke and soon we are drawn away from communion with the Lord to participating in the lusts of the flesh, whether real or imagined. Even songs, perhaps I should say, especially songs can be an extremely dangerous source of ear-pollution.

Isaiah 33:15 cautions us to *stop our ears from hearing of bloodshed.* That rules out most movies and television series and many songs these days! If we eliminate looking at and/or listening to things that pollute our eyes, our ears and our heart, the world would definitely be a different place!

We should sort through what we hear. Discard what doesn't bring peace. I'm by no means saying we shouldn't pray concerning the negatives such as war, drug addiction, alcohol abuse, gangs and such. Definitely pray about these things. Intercession is itself a guard against ear-pollution as well as a guard for our hearts. As a matter of fact, if we go about praying in the spirit, we miss so much of those things that shatter peace.

Here's a scripture that can help us order our thought life and sift what we hear, think and see.

For the rest, brethren, whatever is true, whatever is worthy of reverence and is honorable and seemly, whatever is just, whatever is pure, whatever is lovely and lovable, whatever is kind and winsome and gracious, if there is any virtue and excellence, if there is anything worthy of praise, think on and weigh and take account of these things (fix your minds on them). Practice what you have learned and received and heard and seen in me and model your way of living on it, and the God of peace (of untroubled, undisturbed well-being) will be with you ^{Philippians 4:8-9}.

If we refuse to give thought to the negative or sordid things we hear but choose rather to think about what is good, we will avoid much contention and stress. I'm not saying we should ignore or pretend there is no negative influences or ungodliness in the world. Certainly, those things are everywhere and are matters for prayer. It's what we meditate on—set our minds to that determines our outlook. These should be godly things.

PREPARATION FOR RESURRECTION

25. How can I protect my ears from listening to gossip without damaging relationships?
26. What are ways I can protect my ears from ear pollution when I'm in public places?
27. The benefits to tuning my ears to meditating on the Word of God are:
28. Am I able to hear the voice of God above the voices around me?
29. What are some godly alternatives to fill my ears during commute times?

OUR EYES,
OUR EARS,
ARE PIPELINES TO OUR HEART.
OUR HEART
FEEDS OUR MOUTH
AND DICTATES OUR ACTIONS.

OTHER STEPS WE MAY NEED TO TAKE

We May Have To Let Go Of Some Relationships:

The first time letting go of relationships is mentioned in the Bible is in the second chapter of Genesis verse 24 when Adam said of Eve,

"Therefore a *man shall leave his father and his mother and shall become united and cleave to his wife.*"

Here are a few other examples:

- Cain was sent away from his family by God ^{Genesis 4:9-16}.

- Later we learn that Abram was asked by God to leave his family and go to a land he had never seen. If Abram was willing to go, God promised to make of him a nation and he would be a blessing to all the earth ^{Genesis 12:1-3}.

- Lot and his family separated from Abram and moved into Sodom ^{Genesis 13:8-9}.

- Later the angels separated Lot and his family from that city as well ^{Genesis 19:15-22}.

- Other relationships, some completely abandoned, include:
  - Abraham with Hagar and Ishmael ^{Genesis 21:9-14}.
  - Jacob from his mother and father ^{Genesis 28:1-2}.
  - Jacob and his family from his father-in-law ^{Genesis 31:3}.
  - Joseph when his brothers sold him into slavery ^{Genesis 37:23-28}.
  - Moses from his mother, then later from the palace ^{Exodus 2:1-10; Exodus 2:15}.
  - Jonathan from David ^{1 Samuel 20}.

- Michael from David [2 Samuel 6:20-23].
- Elisha from his family [1 Kings 19:16].
- Saul and Barnabas from the church at Antioch [Acts 13:2-3].

The list could go on and on. Long story short, sometimes for good reasons as well as because of bad relationship, we have to leave some people to be able to move into God's plan for our lives. We may even have to separate from or avoid family members who seem determined to keep us from our purpose and the hope of our future. No! Don't go there. I'm not talking about divorce!

Gossips:

Proverbs is full of instructions concerning relationships. One particular group of people we need to avoid is GOSSIPS!

He who goes about as a talebearer (a gossip) reveals secrets, but he who is trustworthy and faithful in spirit keeps the matter hidden [Proverbs 11:13].

The words of a whisperer or slanderer are like dainty morsels or words of sport (to some, but to others are like deadly wounds); and they go down into the innermost parts of the body or of the victim's nature [Proverbs 18:8 and Proverbs 26:22].

For lack of wood the fire goes out, and where there is no whisperer, contention ceases [Proverbs 26:20].

58

See also Leviticus 19:16 and Proverbs 20:19. There are many more scriptures concerning gossips, slanderers and the like, but I will leave that for your research.

Avoid Angry People:
Have you ever noticed when you are around angry people, you can sense the agitation in the atmosphere? Are you filled enough with righteousness, peace and joy in the Holy Ghost that you are able to turn/reverse the atmosphere, establishing a foothold for the Kingdom of God? Or, do you leave as soon as you can—get away from that person, or— perhaps get caught up in anger yourself ^{Romans 14:17-18}?

Now, it's one thing to "get" angry and another to "stay" angry. Ephesians Chapter 4, verse 26 tells us to be angry but don't sin. It also tells us to not carry anger over into the night, don't take it into the next day. Let it go. Don't be an angry person and don't hang around with angry people.

There is a strong warning in Proverbs 22:24-25 concerning friendship with angry people.

Make no friendship with a man given to anger, and with a wrathful man do not associate, lest you learn his ways and get yourself into a snare.

Too often we think we can help someone understand their need to let go of anger simply by befriending them. However, most often we become infected with their dis-ease. At first it's just a thought, something we want to snap at someone. The next thing we know, we have snapped and hurt someone we love. We have been caught in the snare of an angry man.

Proverbs 29 verse 22 tells us *"A man of wrath stirs up strife, and a man given to anger commits and causes much transgression.*" The word translated "transgression" here can also mean rebellion. Don't be a person who stirs up strife and rebellion and don't hang around with people who do. If they're in your immediate family that can be difficult, but prayer, much prayer can turn the situation. Ask the Lord to give you prayer strategies, declarations and decrees to get this person healed emotionally and delivered from the anger. Also ask for strategies to preserve your own soul from anger.

1 Corinthians chapter 15 verse 33 clearly warns us to "*not be deceived and misled! Evil companionships (communion, associations) corrupt and deprave good manners and morals and character.*" We should find people to associate with who strengthen us in godliness, righteousness, goodness, and peace. People who cause us to want to improve in all facets of our lives and who we can encourage as well.

This scripture is also very important in relationships with those who are Christians in name only. Don't let them influence you into compromise. Don't allow them to corrupt your good manners, morals and character. Actually we're told to not have even lunch with them or wish them God's speed.

- Don't do lunch with them:

    But now I write to you not to associate with anyone who bears the name of (Christian) brother if he is known to be guilty of immorality or greed, or is an idolater (whose soul is devoted to any object that usurps the place of God), or is a person with a foul tongue (railing, abusing, reviling, slandering), or is a drunkard or a swindler or a robber. (No) you must not so much as eat with such a person [1 Corinthians 5:11].

- Don't even wish them God's speed:

If anyone comes to you and does not bring this doctrine (is disloyal to what Jesus Christ taught), do not receive him (do not accept him, <u>do not welcome or admit him) into your house or bid him Godspeed or give him any encouragement</u>. **For he who wishes him success (who encourages him, wishing him Godspeed) is a partaker in his evil doings** ^{2 John 1:10-11}.

LISTEN! We are entering a time in the development of the Body of Christ when we MUST adhere to these warnings and return to holiness. God will not be mocked ^{Galatians 6:7-10}. Living under grace doesn't mean closing our eyes to wrong, not in our lives or in the lives of our associates. James 5:19-20 clearly admonishes us:

My brethren, if anyone among you strays from the Truth and falls into error and another person brings him back to God, let the latter one be sure that whoever turns a sinner from his evil course will save that one's soul from death and will cover a multitude of sins (procure the pardon of the many sins committed by the convert).

We are told in Hebrews 13:17:
Obey your spiritual leaders and submit to them continually recognizing their authority over you, for they are constantly keeping watch over your souls and guarding your spiritual welfare, as men who will have to render an account of their trust. Do your part to let them do this with gladness and not with sighing

and groaning for that would not be profitable to you either.

Ezekiel 33:4-6 carries a stout warning to those who have been given watch-care over us:

. . . whoever hears the sound of the trumpet and does not take warning, and the sword comes and takes him away, his blood shall be upon his own head. He heard the sound of the trumpet and did not take warning; his blood shall be upon himself. But he who takes warning shall save his life.

*But if the watchman sees the sword coming and does not blow the trumpet and the people are not warned, and the sword comes and takes any one of them, he is taken away in and for his perversity and iniquity, but **his blood will I require at the watchman's hand.***

I'm not suggesting that we become "fruit inspectors." I'm not suggesting that we become accusers of the brethren. What I'm talking about is blatant rebellion. You know when you don't really want your kids around someone or you don't want to be seen with a particular person. We really can't change anyone, not even ourselves without the Spirit of God working in us. We like to think we can, but we really can't. Without His "super" on our "natural," our influence is quite limited. However, we are responsible to one another. We all are responsible for our own decisions but we sometimes need to be pulled back from the brink of destruction.

Don't associate with those who won't listen and think they can continue on in habitual sin simply because they carry the name Christian. We would probably be very surprised to discover how many people are encouraged to continue in destructive behavior simply because we "accept" them in our efforts to influence them.

1 Corinthians 11:31 tells us—*For if we searchingly examined ourselves (detecting our shortcomings and recognizing our own condition), we should not be judged and penalty decreed by the divine judgment.*

We need to take time to examine ourselves. If we monitor our own attitudes and actions, we'll be less likely to get pulled in by those who are trapped in their own sins. We will also rescue many who are on the brink of disobedience.

So, while your promise is out of sight and/or your dream is sick or even in the grave, begin examining yourself. Shed the light of God's Word into the deepest, darkest parts of your being. Even shine it in the areas you think may be full of light. Let the Word of God be your plumb line. In the coming chapters, we'll examine character, attitudes, mindsets, generational contributions and many other aspects that make us who we are. You'll need to be ready to take off the kid-gloves, take off your mask, come out from behind your walls and get ready to……

BE HONEST WITH YOURSELF!

Simply guarding your heart, your thoughts, your mouth, your eyes, your ears and your relationships can change the world. If that seems a little too simplistic to you, consider this:

- If everyone who reads this book or attends this seminar applies these principles in the areas over which they are able to exert influence, consider the possibilities for change.

- Change occurs one person at a time. Even when it seems that there has been a mass conversion, each person, individually, made a decision to change. That's how the kingdom of heaven is formed, little by little, one life at a time.

Jesus helped us understand what the kingdom of heaven is like. He gave sufficient examples to ensure that everyone from any walk of life could understand.

- *The kingdom of heaven is like a man which sowed good seed in his field*: Matthew 13:24. (Farmer)
- *The kingdom of heaven is like a grain of mustard seed* Matthew 13:31. (Farmer, Gardner, Homemaker)
- *The kingdom of heaven is like leaven (sour dough) covered over in three measures of meal or flour, till all of it was leavened* Matthew 13:33. (Homemaker, Baker)
- *The kingdom of heaven is like something precious buried in a field* Matthew 13:44. (Treasure Hunter, Landowner)
- *The kingdom of heaven is like a man who is a dealer in search of fine and precious pearls, who, on finding a single pearl of great price, went and sold all he had and bought it* Matthew 13:45-46. (Jeweler, Merchant, Collector)
- *The kingdom of heaven is like a dragnet which was cast into the sea and gathered in fish of every sort.*

When it was full, men . . . . .sorted out the good fish into baskets but the worthless ones they threw away ^{Matthew 13:47}. (Fisherman)

My Favorite:

- *He (Jesus) said to them, "Therefore every teacher and interpreter of the Sacred Writings who has been instructed about and trained for the kingdom of heaven and has become a disciple is like a householder who brings forth out of his storehouse treasure that is new and (treasure that is) old (the fresh as well as the familiar)* ^{Matthew 13:52}. (Teacher, Preacher, Head of a Family, Merchant, etc.)

REMEMBER

The storehouse is our heart from which the treasure is "flung" out to others,

establishing the Kingdom of Heaven one seed at a time.

PREPARATION FOR RESURRECTION

30. How often do I eat with people who wear/claim the name of Christian but who live like the world (in sin and error)?
31. Do I allow people in my house who preach a "different gospel," hoping I can convert them?
32. When someone comes with false doctrine or who I simply don't want in my house and I turn them away at the door, do I wish them "Godspeed"—good luck—blessings?
33. What relationships do I need to eliminate or change?
34. Am I a godly choice for my friends, relatives, children?

Psalms 19:7-11

The law of the lord is perfect, restoring the whole person;
the testimony of the Lord is sure, making wise the simple.
The precepts of the Lord are right, rejoicing the heart;
the commandment of the Lord is pure and bright,
enlightening the eyes.
The reverent fear of the Lord is clean, enduring forever;
the ordinances of the Lord are true and righteous altogether.
More to be desired are they than gold, even than much fine
gold;
they are sweeter also than honey and drippings from the
honeycomb.
Moreover, by them is Your servant warned (reminded,
illuminated, and instructed);
and in keeping them there is great reward.

CHAPTER 4
FOUNDATIONS

*"Our foundations are made up of family values, cultural issues,
thought patterns, our spiritual structure,
the events of our life.
Sometimes, there are hidden
flaws that wreck our future even before we get there.
These things can be changed."*

CHECK YOUR FOUNDATION:

Our foundation is the basis on which we build our lives. Sometimes we carefully build around major flaws in our foundation rather than looking at what caused them and facilitating repair. We may have lived with it for decades looking the other way when its effect is manifested in our life. O.K., I know some of you are not plugging into this at all. Cracks in our foundation are errors in our beliefs, emotional trauma, cultural inhibitions, many other factors that when undealt with inhibit our ability to respond properly to certain difficult issues of life.

I'm not saying we should "dig up our past." However, if our past is keeping us from stepping into our future, we need to deal with it.

GET PAST YOUR PAST!

It's time to put off those old things and put on the newness of life ^{Ephesians 4:22; Colossians 3:9-10}! Once we embrace salvation and come into personal relationship with Jesus Christ, it's time for major renovation. Not only is our identity changed, but also our mind begins the process of renewal and our moral code begins to be re-established. However, if we are not discipled, we often don't know how to proceed. What we need is to be raised to newness of life ^{Romans 6:4}. The main "organ" that needs renovation is our soul.

John says in 3 John 1:2:
Beloved, I pray that you may prosper in every way
and that your body may keep well, even as I know
your soul keeps well and prospers.

Here the word prosper actually means "to grant a prosperous and expeditious journey, to lead by a direct and easy way; to grant a successful issue, to cause to prosper; to prosper, be successful" ^{Strong's #2137}.

LIFE IS A JOURNEY! It isn't staying in one place or condition, being like we've always been. A prospering soul is constantly putting on newness of life, letting go of the old, unprofitable, inhibitive things and stretching into renewal.

Bottom line:
- If we're not prospering and in good health . . .
  - o It may not be a medical condition or a condition of the economy.
    - ▪ We may need to check our soul.

Even if it is a medical condition, the true cause and cure may be tied up in our foundation and how we deal with our day-to-day life:

- How we deal with stress.
- How we communicate with others.
- Where our trust lies.
- Many other things that possibly go back to the beginning of the development of our character—back to our foundation.

Likewise, some of our financial problems are directly connected with our foundation.

- We handle finances the way our parents did or...
- We never learned to handle finances at all and have no understanding of it.
- Possibly, we use poor judgment or need discipline in the area of self control so we take care of first things first.
  - o Obligations/essentials first (things like house and car payments, other contractual items, food, etc.).
  - o Wants and wishes (non-essentials) last.

For many of us, we are not familiar with the scriptural principles that govern health and finances. When applied properly, biblical principles will work for saint and sinner alike ^{Matthew 5:45}. There's nothing better or more effective in restoring cracked foundations than the Word of the Living God.

If we look at the giants of ministry we can find several who died early deaths simply because they did not or were unable to deal with soulish issues. There was a book written a few years ago that examined great spiritual leaders. When I read that book, I really didn't like it. I actually became angry toward the author because he exposed peoples' faults, their weaknesses, their shortcomings, but it certainly has a lesson we need to heed. You learn of people who beat their spouse, had a problem with alcohol, womanizing, etc., and God was still able and willing to use them for His glory. Their lives furthered His Kingdom even though they were not perfect; even though they seemed unwilling or unable to overcome. They actually died quite young.

Then you can look at people, fathers and mothers in the faith, like Oral Roberts, Kenneth Hagin, Joy Dawson, Lester Sumrall, Dr. Criswell, R. W. Schambach, Paul and Jan Crouch, Charles and Frances Hunter, Billy Graham, Peter and Doris Wagner, so many others who prospered even as their souls prospered and were granted long life.

One of my favorite scriptures, Psalm 19:12-14, needs no further amplification. It is one of my prayers for my own life.

Who can discern his lapses and errors? Clear me from hidden and unconscious faults. Keep back Your servant also from presumptuous sins; let them not have dominion over me! Then shall I be blameless, and I shall be innocent and clear of great transgression. Let the words of my mouth and the meditation of my heart be acceptable in Your sight, O Lord, my firm, impenetrable Rock and my Redeemer.
Another of my favorite scriptures is Psalm 51:10:
Create in me a clean heart, O God, and renew a right, persevering, and steadfast spirit within me.

David goes on to say that this request is not just for his personal benefit, but also that he can teach others God's ways and that sinners will be converted. There is always someone watching us and/or listening to us. Wouldn't it be wonderful if what they see teaches them about God's ways and converts sinners?!

Let's look at one more scripture—Psalm 139:23-24 (again):

> *Search me (thoroughly), O God, and know my heart! Try me and know my thoughts! And see if there is any wicked or hurtful way in me, and lead me in the way everlasting.*

Here the word "wicked" actually means pain or sorrow. It can also mean "idol" [Strong's #6990]. So—is there pain or sorrow in your heart? Is there an idol that's twisting your judgment and/or obscuring your vision?

I'm sure you've heard it said, "Hurting people hurt people." We don't mean to, but it seems unavoidable. We often don't even know we've hurt someone. When we hurt, we respond to others out of our hurt. Then they are hurt so the pain is propagated. Be willing to take your hurts to the Lord. Talk to someone you can trust. Openly acknowledge what's bothering you so they can pray for you so you can be healed [James 5:16].

Are there idols?

- TV:

- o Even Christian television can be a distraction and can easily become an idol.
- Self:
  - o We could write an entire book on how self can become an idol.
- Our beliefs:
  - o If we have a belief that causes us to have a superior or an inferior attitude, we need to look at the validity of that belief and/or the fullness of our understanding of it.
- Our heart:
  - o If it harbors pride or insecurity it can cause us to lift our self up and make us ineffective.
- Our love level:
  - o When we are loving out of a pure heart, we won't be puffed up.
    - We must allow the love that God has shed abroad in our hearts to reach out and touch others [Romans 5:5].
    - Yes, we may be on a fast track with God but we can't keep running with the horses [Jeremiah 12:5] if we don't keep our love tank full.
    - Love doesn't push itself forward.
      - o Study 1 Corinthians 13.

GET TO KNOW LOVE OUTSIDE THE SOULISH
REALM.
GET TO KNOW TRUE LOVE—GOD STYLE.

*The love of God is shed abroad/poured out in our hearts
by the Holy Ghost*

which is given unto us ^{Romans 5:5}.

So, this is what I mean by checking your foundation.
- Are there "issues" you can't or are not willing to see and get past?
- Do certain people seem to know where your "buttons" are and they know how to push them?
- Do you often say, "That's the way I've always been?"
  o Is that really good enough for you?
    ▪ Does how you've always been look better than how you could be?
      • Does it look anything like Jesus?
- Are there attitudes or reactions you catch yourself in the middle of that you wouldn't want your spiritual leaders or Jesus to see?
  o For instance…
    ▪ Sudden anger.
    ▪ A "little" lie.
    ▪ "Accidentally" picking up something that belongs to someone else.
      • Maybe it belongs to the company you work for and they won't miss it.
- Are you still hurting or being offended by something that happened in your childhood?
  o Maybe someone touched you wrong.
  o Maybe you were even molested or raped.
    ▪ There truly is healing, even for that, in forgiveness.
    ▪ No. Probably you won't forget but as you allow Holy Spirit to work forgiveness in you…

- You can be healed.
- You can be made whole.
  - The pain will stop.

Please don't think I'm treating this lightly. I've been there. I understand. It isn't easy to go on. Interestingly, it isn't easy to submit ourselves to what it takes to become whole again. But I promise, it is well worth the time and effort. Please give yourself a chance.

I highly recommend <u>The Three Battlegrounds</u> by Francis Frangipane and <u>The Wounded Heart</u> by Dr. Dan B. Allender. These two books were key to my healing. Joyce Myer also has a very good book dealing with these issues—<u>The Battlefield of The Mind</u>. It's also available as tape, CD and DVD series.

Do you get angry just because someone is angry with you? Do you automatically defend yourself? That's the spirit of offense! It will rob your peace and your ability to influence others to any degree of effectiveness. It will rob you of valuable relationships.

If possible, as far as it depends on you, live at peace with everyone. Beloved, never avenge yourselves, but leave the way open for God's wrath; for it is written, "Vengeance is Mine, I will repay (requite)," says the Lord Romans 12:18-19.

Maybe you feel people simply don't respect you. Do you respect yourself? We carry a "climate" around with us—an atmosphere if you will. People know when we don't respect ourselves. Our attitude toward ourselves breeds that attitude in those with whom we have to do, especially outside Christian circles.

- Make a list of things you like about yourself.
- Make a list of things you don't like about yourself.
- Begin consciously eliminating the list of things you don't like by replacing them with the desired opposite.
- When possible, find scripture to base the new attribute on.
  o Building everything on biblical principles solidifies and strengthens the decision to change as well as the lasting effect.
- Prayer draws God into the equation and enlists the aid of Holy Spirit.
- Maybe you are in the habit of complaining. Check out what the Children of Israel did that was so displeasing to God Numbers 14:29, Numbers 16:41-45, Psalm 106:21-27, 1 Corinthians 10:8-11.
  o He didn't like their murmuring and complaining.
  o He doesn't like ours any more than He liked theirs.
- Maybe you feel taken advantage of and . . .
  o "No one's going to do that to me again!"
- Maybe you just don't know how to submit to authority.
  o Or maybe you think no one has the right to tell you what to do.
    ▪ Same thing.
- Maybe you have low self esteem.
  o Find out why!

75

- If you perceive someone is in a better position than you...
  o Press in!!!
    ▪ It may simply mean they have been able to spend more time in His presence than you have.
    ▪ It may mean that they didn't have to work through the muck and mire you've been working through.
    ▪ It may mean their challenges were even more difficult than yours.
    ▪ It may mean their call is different than yours.
    ▪ It may mean they have fewer distractions in their life than you do—family, job, commitment, finances.
    ▪ It may mean their heritage gave them an advantage.
    ▪ It may even mean you don't know everything about them. What they're struggling with.
- Let me strongly encourage you:
  o Whatever the reason(s) for differences in development or position, love yourself enough to be self-examining, honest with yourself, and motivated enough to make necessary changes to reach your goal.

PRESS IN!

Your life and accomplishments are not going to look exactly like anyone else.

- They don't have your personality.
- They don't have your relationship with THE VINE!

- Even if they've been through what you've been through,
    - They didn't handle it the same way because. . .
        - They Are Not You!

Although none of these things are simple or easy, they are not game stoppers. You can overcome.
- You may need healing.
- You may need soul renovation.
- You may need deliverance.
    - Maybe even from yourself.

The thing is, once we think we're fixed, made whole, perfected, someone finds another button to push. Or, we find something in ourselves we know isn't godly and He would not approve of. We need to be watchful, guard our righteousness. It is imputed but we can certainly soil it.

So, if you have a crack in your foundation it may go back to childhood. Such a crack may go back to your parents, or even back to your grandparents. The thing is, you must look at what's holding you in place:
- UNTIL WE ARE WILLING to look at ourselves,
- UNTIL WE ARE WILLING to change our attitudes,
- UNTIL WE ARE WILLING to be completely honest with ourselves and others......

WE CAN FLOUNDER AROUND IN THE WILDERNESS OF FAILURE AND BURIED DREAMS AND NEVER WALK IN THE FULLNESS OF OUR CALL,

OR COME INTO THE FULLNESS OF OUR PROMISE.

Some Authors and Speakers I Highly Recommend for
Character Development:

Chuck Pierce

T. D. Jakes

Rick Joyner

John Maxwell

James Goll

Steven Covey

Bill Johnson

Joyce Meyer

Rick Warren

Kenneth Copeland

Gloria Copeland

Barbara Wentroble

Duane Sheriff

Paul Keith Davis

Mike Murdock

John Eckhardt

Peter Wagner

Watchman Nee

There are many others who base character structure on
biblical principles. Find one from whom you can receive and
apply the principles they present.

PREPARATION FOR RESURRECTION

1. Have I passed the test of my past?
   - If so, how am I changed for the better?
   - If not, what steps can I take to overcome?

2. What pushes my buttons?
3. What do I need to deal with to disconnect those buttons?
4. Am I still angry?
5. Am I willing to forgive?
6. Is there a root of bitterness?
7. Do I blame others?
8. Have I accepted responsibility for my own attitude no matter what was done to me or by whom?
9. Do I need outside help?
   - Pastoral counseling?
   - Support group?
   - A close friend?
10. Things I don't like about myself include:
11. I can become more "self-friendly" by...

PSALM 51:7-13

Purify me with Hyssop,
And I shall be [ceremonially] clean;
Wash me and I shall [in reality] be whiter than snow.
Make me to hear joy and gladness and be satisfied;
Let the bones which You have broken rejoice.
Hide Your face from my sins and blot out all my guilt and
iniquities.
Create in me a clean heart, O God,
And renew a right, persevering, and steadfast spirit within
me.
Cast me not away from Your presence
And take not Your Holy Spirit from me.
Restore to me the joy of Your salvation
And uphold me with a willing spirit.
Then will I teach transgressors Your ways,
And sinners shall be converted and return to You.

CHAPTER 5
A CLOSER LOOK

*"The Word of God
IS
the fulcrum
to a balanced life"*

One of the most difficult things for me to deal with and the thing that held me back the most was INDEPENDENCE! I was really good at independence. I learned how to work on my house, how to fix plumbing. I learned roofing. I could paint with the best of them. I even learned how to work on my own car!

I know there is a fine line here. We need to move from "dependent" as when we were young children, to independent where we are whole and healed, then on to "interdependent." Interdependent means inter-relating in such a way that we are benefited while being a benefit to others. We need to be in a place where our spiritual, emotional, mental, physical and material well-being is not entirely dependent on someone else so we can make choices that are not based on need. In that place, we are able to reach out and take a risk to benefit someone else. We cannot be truly whole without one another. We are one body, one in Christ and members one with another ^{Romans 12:5}.

I had no problem moving from dependent to independent, but I crossed the line. I not only crossed the line, I built a fortress there and set up housekeeping! I didn't need anyone! At one time, I even told God, "I'll give you my life and everything that concerns, but never ask me to give up my independence again."

IMAGINE THAT! The mud telling the Potter what it's willing to do and be. I'm sure you never did that. Well, if you know the Lord you know what He required of me. I did give up my independence. I came to a place I could not go on without someone helping me. I went through a short period of time, about two years, during which I was totally dependent again. I was not only financially dependent, but also needing a place to live and food for my belly. I became emotionally bankrupt. My spiritual life grew at an exceptional rate because God truly was my refuge. His presence was my sanctuary and His Word my daily bread. However, there came a time when that was not enough.

The Lord told me I was dying. I had a broken spirit. Proverbs 15:13 and 17:22 tell us that sorrow of heart breaks the spirit and a broken spirit dries the bones or strength ^{Strong's #1634}.

I was still ministering. I had a small "inner circle" who were allowed to touch me only as I permitted—and I didn't permit anything beyond their receiving from me. That was not enough to sustain my soul. The Lord told me they were my life support team and I had been too long on life support—too long giving and not permitting myself to receive. I was beginning to die.

The Lord told me to commit to a church pastored by people I barely knew. Let me tell you, if you haven't experienced unconditional love and nurturing, you have missed an awesome, enriching, life-changing experience. These people knew how to love. They chiseled me out of my self-imposed tomb and taught me how to live again.

We simply cannot make it on our own…alone…with no input from a love relationship of some sort. That's not God's plan. It's not good for man to be alone ^{Genesis 2:18}. That statement is not gender specific. It's not good for woman either! Mankind was built for interrelationship. That doesn't mean we have to be married though various studies indicate people live longer and healthier when married. It simply means we need to be tied to someone in a covenant relationship. Giving love and not receiving love soon brings a soul to bankruptcy. A bankrupt soul neither gives or receives. Interestingly, it is possible to die of loneliness.

- Find two people:
  - One who can strengthen you.
  - One to whom you can be a strength.
    - Then, begin practicing needing and being needed.

Let's look at Ecclesiastes 4:9-13:
Two are better than one, because they have a good (more satisfying) reward for their labor; for if they fall, the one will lift up his fellow. But woe to him who is alone when he falls and has not another to lift him up!

Again, if two lie down together, then they have warmth; but how can one be warm alone?

And though a man might prevail against him who is alone, two will withstand him. A threefold cord is not quickly broken.

Better is a poor and wise youth than an old and foolish king who no longer knows how to receive counsel (friendly reproof and warning) even though (the youth) comes out of prison to reign, while the other, born a king, becomes needy.

You see? Even kings and rulers need to have someone who can correct them. They need someone who can comfort them, counsel them, just listen to them. They need people to rule over, people to lead, soldiers to train, accountants to count their money! More importantly than anything else, kings and rulers need interpersonal relationships, just like you and me.

Proverbs 11:14 tells us: *Where no wise guidance is, the people fall,* **but in the multitude of counselors there is** *safety.*

PEOPLE – WE NEED EACH OTHER!

So you say, "I've always been a loner." That was once me. After we graduated, my lifelong best friend told me she had always admired me because I didn't need anyone. Interestingly, I admired her because she did need people. Loners can't touch people. Loners don't allow others to touch them. If what you've always been or what you've always done doesn't work anymore, it's time for a change!

- You don't have to be in charge all the time.

- o Team up with others.
- o Learn to give as well as take.
  - ■ I'm not talking materialistically.
- You don't have to be honored all the time.
  - o Find ways to honor others.

Let's look at Romans 12:10 and dissect some of the words so we gain a deeper understanding of this scripture.

(Be kindly affectioned KJV) Love one another with brotherly affection (as members of one family), giving precedence and showing honor to one another.

- That word "affectioned" in the King James Version means:
  - o Loving affection, prone to love, loving tenderly; used chiefly of the reciprocal tenderness of parents and children Strong's #5387.
- "Honor" actually means:
  - o A valuing by which the price is fixed; hence the price itself: of the price paid or received for a person or thing bought or sold.
  - o Honor which belongs or is shown to one: the honor which one has by reason of rank and state of office which he holds; deference, reverence Strong's #5092.
- "Preferring" means:
  - o to go before and show the way, to go before and lead, to go before as a leader Strong's #4285.

Let someone else have the spotlight:
- o Be kindly affectioned.

- ○ Honor one another.
- ○ Prefer one another.
  - ▪ See how many people you can put in the spotlight or share the spotlight with.
    - • You could change a life!
- • Don't be offended if someone doesn't recognize your gifts or your office.
  - ○ But, be sure you recognize theirs!
    - ▪ I know you know this, but we can only lead by serving.
    - ▪ Make sure others recognize Jesus in you.

We are told in 1 Corinthians 14:29-32:

*So let two or three prophets speak (those inspired to preach or teach), while the rest pay attention and weigh and discern what is said. **But if an inspired revelation comes to another who is sitting by, then let the first one be silent.** For in this way you can give testimony (prophesying and thus interpreting the divine will and purpose) one by one, so that all may be instructed and all may be stimulated and encouraged; for **the spirits of the prophets (the speakers in tongues) are under the speaker's control and subject to being silenced as may be necessary**.*

Don't be afraid to examine and test yourself:

Examine and test and evaluate your own selves *to see whether you are holding to your faith and showing the proper fruits of it.* ***Test and prove yourselves*** *(not Christ).* ***Do you not yourselves realize and know thoroughly by an ever increasing***

experience that Jesus Christ is in you unless you are (counterfeits) disapproved on trial and rejected ² Corinthians 13:5₂

Emphasis has been added in the above scripture. It is so full of guidance and wisdom! This is a good "mirror scripture." It could be displayed strategically throughout our homes. If we can get this Word living in our hearts, it could improve family relations and change cities—even the world.

WOW! We are to examine and test, evaluate and prove ourselves! Take note! Christ is being formed in us ^{Galatians 4:19}! We need to look at ourselves closely! Make sure we're co-operating with Holy Spirit, the One Who forms Christ in us! Once we've been weaned from the milk of the Word, we should begin searching out the meat of the Word ^{Hebrews 5:12-14}. Sometimes we have to go back to the milk when there are divisions, envy and strife in us ^{1 Corinthians 3:2-3}. But Paul says we should get past that.

In Hebrews 5:13-6:2 he says that if we're still on milk we are *unskilled in the doctrine of righteousness (of conformity to the divine will in purpose, thought and action).* He says we are *mere infants, not even able to talk yet.* But the meat—*solid food is for grown-ups, those whose senses and mental faculties are trained by practice to discriminate and distinguish between what is morally good and noble and what is evil and contrary either to divine or human law.* We are to grow up *and get past the elementary stage in the teachings and doctrine of Christ (the Messiah),* **advancing steadily toward the completeness and perfection that belong to spiritual maturity.** *Let us not be laying again the* *foundation of repentance and abandonment of dead works (dead formalism) and the faith by which you turned to God, with teachings about purifying, the laying on of hands, the resurrection from the dead, and eternal judgment and punishment.* He says it's time to move on to advanced teaching ^{Hebrews 6:3}!

THE WORD OF GOD
IS
THE FULCRUM
TO A BALANCED LIFE.

PREPARATION FOR RESURRECTION

1. Where am I in my development? Am I happy and able to function fully even when I'm alone or do I need someone all the time?

2. Am I too independent? (I don't need anyone else in my life, or—I don't want anyone intruding in my life.)
   - If so, is there woundedness?
   - Is there repressed anger?
   - Are there issues from my past that keep me an island?
   - Do I have an aversion to authority (nobody's going to tell me what to do)?
   - Do I need to prove that I can "do all things" on my own?
   - Am I just so "super-human" I simply don't need anyone and don't need to be needed?

3. Am I willing to let someone else reach out and touch me even if it's just for their benefit?

- Am I willing and able to be benefited by such a touch?
4. How can I open up to allow interaction with others?
5. Am I totally dependent on someone else in any area of my life?
6. Do I need someone around to "make me happy?"
   - Has anyone ever been able to really make me happy?
   - If so, what do I do just for them without thinking of benefit to myself?
   - What wounds need to be healed so I can be whole and happy?
7. Am I totally financially dependent on someone else?
   - If so, how can I be a benefit to them?
   - What can I begin doing to begin gaining some level of independence?
8. Am I totally dependent on someone else to assure a roof over my head?
9. Am I at a place in my life where I contribute to the lives of those around me simply because I want to participate in the fullness of life with others as well as allowing them to participate in my life?
10. How can I more positively affect my surroundings, people, places and things?
11. How can I promote more positive interaction with others, being a benefit to them, while allowing them to benefit my life?
12. Who in my life is a strength to me and how do they strengthen me?
13. To whom am I a strength and how do I strengthen them?

14. I need someone in my life who......
15. I can touch people positively by......
16. Here are five people I can honor: (Make a list. Some suggestions...husband, wife, parent, child, friend, protégé, pastor, teacher, etc.)
    - I can honor them by...(List ways to honor each individually.)

CHAPTER 6
WHAT IS LOVE?

*"Love isn't just a word. Love isn't really a feeling.
To truly live is to love.
Love is life and life abundantly."*

I'll be honest with you, this has been a major problem for me from time to time. At one time, I loved everybody and everything. People called me Pollyanna and Unsinkable Molly Brown. Then the fiery darts began piercing my armor. I actually lost the capacity to love anyone or anything except a precious little dog. When I think of the darkness of my soul with only the spark of love to embrace a little dog, well—it's indescribable how cold and empty you can become. I am very grateful that little dog, Charity, was in my life keeping the spark of life alive through love. Thank You, Lord.

It took a long time and a lot of dying to self to be willing and able to choose to trust and love. Walls had to be torn down. I had to experience vulnerability. That was a tough one. No. It wasn't easy nor was it something I did willingly, though I knew it was something I needed to do. I began with,

"Lord, I'm willing to be willing for You to change me by Your Spirit."

I chose to examine myself and make changes in me—changes in attitudes, changes in associations. I had to take chances with people and relationships until finally I'm able to experience and show love again. I'm finally wanting to reach out and love other people. To get here, I had to first trust God—again. NO! It wasn't "learning" to trust Him. He had proven Himself to me. He has never failed me nor forsaken me. I had to **choose** to trust Him.

I had to trust Him to not put anything on me or allow anything to come upon me or into my life without His love to enable me. He talked to me for three years about restoration of the family. I simply would not trust Him to not restore those relationships through which I had experienced things beyond my capacity to cope with. Once I chose to permit restoration of family, even if it meant reuniting me with those I could not imagine trusting again, He began enlarging my capacity to love.

Since that time I have been reunited with my three living siblings just before two of them entered heaven's gate. And, He's given me brothers and sisters, mothers and fathers, cousins, aunts and uncles within the Body of Christ. He promises to "set the solitary in families" Psalm 68:6; Mark 10:29-30. I have found Him to be faithful in all His ways and true to His Word Psalm 19:7-11.

Even when I was unable to love, My Lord surrounded me with people who would not stop loving me. I could have become a recluse, but He would not permit it. He set me smack dab in the middle of a house that was home to not only people with an extended family of kids and grandkids, but cats, dogs, and as well! There was no escape for me! I had to allow His love to flow through them to me. It was contagious and I soon began loving back. Isn't He something!? I will ever be grateful to Cindy and Knox for completely accepting me and loving me when I was so unlovable. They embraced me as a family member.

Lillian, who was used by Holy Spirit on numerous occasions to prevent me from returning to darkness and danger...is a true sister. You've always been there for me. I believe you saved my life as you were led by Holy Spirit to not only intercede but to intervene. Your love has been a wonder to me. Your acceptance of me...your prayers for me. Where would I be had you not been in my life? Thank you that you and Merv have opened your home to me on numerous occasions as if I were truly one of the family. God is so good, may He continually bless and prosper you!

Alan, always willing to come to my aid, even when it was inconvenient, is to this day, a true brother. You listened, literally, hours on end as I poured the poison out of my heart. Never once did you judge me. You always had time for me. Money could not have purchased the counseling that your unconditional love and acceptance afforded me.

Fran, I have seen you put your life on hold for my sake. You have believed in me beyond my ability to believe in myself. You have sacrificed in many ways to assure I had what I needed to press into God's plan for my life. You committed yourself to my success and did everything you could to make me "happen." You have sown into every area of my life. When the pain of life was crushing me, you were the stop check that kept me from closing the door on love.

David and Barbara, your generosity with love and acceptance rescued me when I didn't want to be rescued. I'm so very grateful you did not let go of me. You were water to my soul.

I know there are some of you reading this book who really don't know how to allow yourself to be loved, let alone reach out and love others. I've shared these things with you so you will know I understand. One of the most interesting things in my life has been the change God worked in my heart when I finally surrendered. I didn't surrender to the circumstances of my life. I didn't surrender to people, family or friends. I didn't even surrender to myself. I knew I wasn't trustworthy. I would hurt myself again. I surrendered to My Father. The very moment I said, "Father, I choose to trust you," I felt joy for the first time in years. True joy rushed into my heart the moment I reopened the door to Father God.

The Lord never left me. He didn't walk out on me. I don't even remember when I stopped trusting Him. I do know it was difficult to recognize that I really did not trust Him and that excluding people from my heart excluded Him as well.

You, too, really can love again. You can actually allow yourself to be loved again. It truly is a matter of trusting God. Trust Him from whom love comes. I know! I can hear you saying right now, "I trust GOD! It's all the people I don't trust." But there's a mystery here. If we're harboring anger, bitterness, unforgiveness, or distrust toward people, the bottom line is, it's because we're not trusting God [1 John 3:17; 4:20-21].

HE IS WELL ABLE TO:

- Heal us, enable us, deliver us, give us discernment, comfort us, teach us and guide us.
- Be whatever we allow Him to be in our lives.
- Re-introduce us to real, true love.

The wonderful thing about my time in darkness is <u>God's love was still at work in me</u>. He loves us even when we're unlovable and unable to love! We should never underestimate the POWER of HIS LOVE.

He had already shed His love abroad in my heart ^{Romans 5:5}, though I could not experience the love of other people, God's love was at work in me and even manifesting through me. While I was in the dark valley, ministries were born, ministers were affirmed and trained, people were encouraged. Teachings were developed. There were even signs, wonders and miracles. People were physically and emotionally healed. Souls were delivered from satan's grasp. The Gifts of the Spirit grew in me and in those around me.

All of this simply because God's love was working in me and manifesting through me as He continued working things out of me—healing me. As one of my sister minister's stated, "God's love is like a seed planted in the ground. There was the dying in the Valley of the Shadow of Death. There was the burial as your ability to experience love was covered over with grief. Then! There was the power of resurrection as God's Love manifested in and through you!"

When we learn to trust God with our heart, our emotions, our soul—everything we are—His love will seep in and so change us and we won't even know when or how it happened. Suddenly, we will realize we are able to both give and receive love. When God's love rules, we find we are able to offer love and we are able to trust. We are able to want to be loved. We are able to experience joy and peace again.

We are nothing without experiencing both sides of love, the giving and the receiving. We can't represent Jesus without walking in love. We can't carry the glory He gave us without loving others. But guess what! He loves us even when we're unlovable and unable to love!!! He loves us through the mess!

According to 1 Corinthians 13:1, we are nothing without love:

If I can speak in the tongues of men and even of angels, but have not love (that reasoning, intentional, spiritual devotion such as is inspired by God's love for and in us), I am only a noisy gong or a clanging cymbal.

We need to discuss something else here as well. What love is not:

- Love isn't always having your way.
- Love isn't being a doormat.
- Love isn't "never having to say you're sorry."
- Love isn't always saying yes.
- Love isn't never expressing your opinion.
- Love isn't being a punching bag.
- Love isn't many things we may have been led to believe love's expression is.

Relationships cannot be built on what another person can do to make us happy or even what we can do to make them happy, whether or not we expect them to reciprocate. All of that is self-centeredness.

Relationships can't be expected to complete us. We need to be whole and happy going into the relationship. When we do enter into covenantal relationship, we both must be allowed to become one with that other person without giving up who and what we are. Both must continue growing, maturing, giving, and receiving. That is inter-dependence— inter-relationship.

Start a relationship the way you can maintain it. Someone once said, "Start out the way you can hold out." Don't pretend to be something you're not. The only way to maintain is to be who you are. Don't try to be who and/or what you think someone may want you to be. Don't try to be "how you've always been." That won't work with or without another person in your life. Yesterday isn't good enough for today. Today, be new and improved by what you learned yesterday, but maintaining the sure foundation of continual scriptural development.

When you do change make sure what is changing is not diminishing your true self. If we are whole independently, think how much better we can be if we learn to be inter-independent while partnered with another independently whole person who is committed to partnering inter-dependently with us!

America is full of "shrinking" women and men who eventually become invisible because they give up who they are, losing themselves to become who they think someone wants or expects them to be. All too often relationships fail because when the new wears off, we begin to be who we really are. When we put our best foot forward, the next part of the step is to put the other foot forward—presenting our entire self.

This is true, especially in marriage. Men marry women for who we present ourselves to be just as we marry men for who they present to us. How tragic it is when one or both find out they are no longer married to the person they fell in love with because that person didn't really exist. Even more tragic is when we find we no longer know how to be the person we were created to be. We've lost our true self while trying to please others—to make something false appear real.

We need to learn who we are and BE who we are. Of equal importance is to allow those around us to be who they are. I'm not talking about tolerating destructive behavior or immorality in yourself or others. I'm talking about being true to yourself and encouraging others to be true to their self, always pressing toward excellence of character.

Look at 1 Corinthians 2:4-5:
And my language and my message were not set forth in persuasive (enticing and plausible) words of wisdom, but they were in demonstration of the Holy Spirit and power, a proof by the Spirit and power of God, operating on me and stirring in the minds of my hearers, the most holy emotions and thus persuading them, So that your faith might not rest in the wisdom of men (human philosophy), but in the power of God.

Paul was not trying to build himself a reputation or to make everyone love and respect him. His aim was that everyone know God and accept Jesus Christ as Savior and Lord. Paul was just as persistent and passionate as a follower of Jesus as he had been a persecutor of the church before the Damascus road experience ^{Acts 9:4-6}. Paul's complete outlook was changed just as his name was changed from Saul to Paul. His focus changed. He began doing exactly opposite of what he had done before. But, his passion, his zeal, his boldness were the same. His true self was redirected, not lost. This can be such a wonderful lesson to us all.

Find A Mentor / Be A Mentor

One of the greatest joys of life is understanding mentorship. Mentorship takes various forms. I found a simple but concise definition through Wikipedia. "Mentorship refers to a personal developmental relationship in which a more experienced or more knowledgeable person helps a less experienced or less knowledgeable person" (en.wikipedia.org/ wiki/Mentorship).

Mentorship also encompasses accountability for our continued progress. Mentors are not normally gentle folk nor are they bullies. They are not interested in how much you enjoy the process or whether you like them or not. Mentors are interested in you becoming a success in whatever facet of life you have sought their help. They are normally bottom-line honest with you. They won't "pet" your flesh so you feel comfortable. They challenge you, always with your success in mind. They perform a godly service in your life.

When you are choosing a mentor:
- Don't look for someone with whom you have a lot in common.
- Don't look for someone to whom you can relate as a father or mother.

- Don't even look for a big brother or sister.
- A good friend is not good enough.
- Someone who has the same weaknesses as you is not to be considered.

Look for someone who is where you want to go, and who is strong enough to reprove, rebuke and exhort you [2 Timothy 4:2]. You can have more than one mentor, but you really need to be consistent with these men and women of God.

I suggest that you choose two mentors:

- One you can interface with personally and on a regular basis. Perhaps a minister or ministry leader with whom you meet for instruction on a regular basis.
- The second should be one whose books, tapes/CD's, blogs, newsletters and conferences feed you.
  - Perhaps your personal mentor has such resources available, though often, this would be another person.
    - It's sort of like main course and desert.

Now, you can overdo conferences but I do recommend them. Conferences take you out of your everyday world. You are able to focus, and the atmosphere is filled with the miracle of single-mindedness (a group of people of one mind) which enables you to experience deeper revelation as well as receive impartation.

When we connect ourselves with those who teach us and strengthen us, we become heirs to their anointings. I have heard this referred to as "Trans-generational Manifestation."

- When Kenneth Copeland began in ministry, he was told he sounded just like Oral Roberts.
- A Pastor where I sometimes attend church often sounds just like Creflo Dollar. Other times he sounds like Charles Stanley.
- I've heard it said that Benny Hinn acts and sounds just like Kathryn Kuhlman.

Who you follow determines your spiritual inheritance. So, choose carefully. Don't follow someone who doesn't show you something to reach for or someone with whom you have faults and/or weaknesses in common.
- Find someone who challenges you to be better than you are.
- Someone who stretches you and causes you to increase in wisdom, knowledge and understanding.
- Someone who is established in the field where you're called and who is prospering in soul and health as well as in their finances [3 John 1:2].
  - These things go together in a person who is advancing in the Kingdom of God.
    - Because they're examining themselves, making sure there are no hidden sins, no hurtful ways, no unforgiveness...
    - Pressing toward the mark for the high call—the supreme and heavenly prize [Philippians 3:14]...
      - Thus enabling God to establish His covenant with them [Deuteronomy 8:18].
        - They will challenge you to do the same.

Now, support those people. Open your resources—your house, your pocketbook and your time to them. Spend time in their company when possible.

In 2 Kings 4, we find it is an honor when a man or woman of God stays at your house. Here the Lord refers to ministers as laborers and the host as one who has hired them even though the minister may have come to preach to the entire city. Jesus tells His disciples when we go into a city and into a house *stay on in the same house, eating and drinking what they provide, for the laborer is worthy of his wages. Do not keep moving from house to house* ^{Luke 10:5-7}.

These days, many ministers stay in hotels when possible so hosting your mentor may not be feasible. Perhaps you can't send monthly offerings to them, but there are many other ways to "support" them.

- Prayer support is vital to everyone, especially those piercing the darkness for others.
- You can also support them by buying their books and tapes and encouraging others to do so. Galatians 6:6 tells us, *"Let him who receives instruction in the Word of God share (communicate) all good things with his teacher (contributing to his support).*
- The word "communicate" here means to join yourself to, become partner or partaker with, to come into communion or fellowship with ^{Strong's #2841}.
- So, we need to see that they partake of what we have to offer as we are partaking of what they have to offer.

These relationships should not be casual. Even though they may not know you by name or by sight, they are feeding you Living Bread. You need to help them any way you can.

Of course, support them financially when you can. You may volunteer at some of their functions. You may buy their materials to share with others. Do find some way to partner with them, some way to contribute to their support.

Let me encourage you a little here: Isaiah 33:14-17 posses an interesting question and answer.

THE QUESTION:

The sinners in Zion are afraid; trembling seizes the godless ones. They cry, **"Who among us can dwell with that devouring fire? Who among us can dwell with those everlasting burnings?."**

THE ANSWER

He who walks righteously and speaks uprightly, who despises gain from fraud and from oppression, who shakes his hand free from the taking of bribes, who stops his ears from hearing of bloodshed and shuts his eyes to avoid looking upon evil.

Such a man will dwell on the heights; his place of defense will be the fortress of rocks; his bread will be given him: water for him will be sure.

Your eyes will see the King in His beauty; your eyes will behold a land of wide distances that stretches afar.

In other words, those who live beyond the norm. Those who stretch past what is acceptable to embrace what is exceptional. Those who choose to live a life beyond mediocrity. Those who live beyond the book. Those who live in relationship.

The Apostle Paul is one who went past the book into relationship. He is significant to us because he did not know Jesus personally before the resurrection. Paul's first encounter with Jesus was on the road to Damascus. As I'm sure you know, at that time his name was Saul. He's like us. We, too, need an encounter with Jesus. As a matter of fact, encounters with Jesus should be a regular experience for us. Yes, even today it is possible. This is what 2 Corinthians 12:2-7 is about. Paul is speaking.

I know a man in Christ who fourteen years ago—whether in the body or out of the body I do not know, God knows—was caught up to the third heaven. And I know that this man—whether in the body or away from the body I do not know, God knows—was caught up into paradise, and he heard utterances beyond the power of man to put into words, which man is not permitted to utter. Of this same man's experiences I will boast, but of myself (personally) I will not boast, except as regards my infirmities (my weaknesses).
Should I desire to boast, I shall not be a witless braggart, but I shall be speaking the truth. But, I abstain from it, so that no one may form a higher estimate of me than is justified by what he sees in me or hears from me. And to keep me from being puffed up and too much elated by the exceeding greatness (preeminence) of these revelations, there was given me a thorn (a splinter) in the flesh, a messenger of satan, to rack and buffet and harass me, to keep me from being excessively exalted.

We are coming to a place in time where we must learn to walk in the Spirit—not just in word but in deed, in every area of our lives. The harvest cannot be brought in by natural means. The angels have been assigned to assist us. Look in Hebrews 1:14:

Are not the angels all ministering spirits (servants) sent out in the service of God for the assistance of those who are to inherit salvation?

We are the heirs of salvation. Don't neglect the assistance He sends to enable you to do the impossible.

We must develop a true relationship with our Lord. We must know our God and Father intimately.

- He will put his Spirit within us [Ezekiel 36:27; John 14:16-17].
- Holy Spirit must be our closest friend [Proverbs 18:24].
  o He is our Comforter, Counselor, Helper, Intercessor, Advocate, Strengthener, and Standby [John 14:16].
- The Lord will lead us into all truth [John 16:13, 14:26].
- He will guide us in all our ways—make straight and plain our paths [Proverbs 3:6].
- He will correct, discipline, and admonish us [Deuteronomy 4:36].
- Holy Spirit will connect us with our Lord and our Father [John 15:26].
- He will give us a new heart [Ezekiel 36:26-27].
- He will speak through us [2 Samuel 23:2].
- We must not be satisfied to just read about Him. We must know and love Him [Job 42:5; John15]!

- We must learn to hear the whispering of the heart of God [1 Kings 19:12; Isaiah 30:21].

- We must learn to relate on His level—getting out of mere humanity [Acts 8:26-40; Revelation 4:1].

- We must walk beyond the Book (the Bible) into relationship. (The Bible is replete with accounts of people who lived in just such a way. As a matter of fact—the Bible is their stories. Even before the cross many lived a supernatural life. AND People expected such of their leaders.)

- Don't just know scripture, know the God of scripture [Job 42:5; John 14:23].

- Know the Author and Finisher of our faith [Hebrews 12:2].

- Know the great I AM [Exodus 3:14; John 8:58, 11:25].

- Know Jesus as if you lived with Him every day for truly you/we do [Hebrews 13:5].

- In John 14, Jesus tells us that if we really love Him, He will send Holy Spirit to be with us forever and He and the Father will make their abode, their special dwelling place in us.

Know the Bible. Meditate on scripture day and night. He will be revealed to you as you apply yourself to pursue Him. I know you work. I understand work. When I was employed in the secular world, periodically during the day, there were moments when what I was doing did not require the concentration of my brain, so I would recall a scripture or pray in tongues, quietly. For example, times like straightening my desk, hanging up my coat, getting a cup of coffee. Yes, many people thought I was a little radical, but they didn't run from me. I didn't try to convert everyone except by the demonstration of my love for God and His for me.

I was working for my employer as unto The Lord, giving them eight hours work for eight hours pay ^{Colossians 3:22-24}. I tried to live before them in such a way that Jesus was demonstrated in my life. I wasn't really good at it all the time. I had too much pain and woundedness buried within. But I tried. I'm still learning to live beyond myself so others can see Him in what I do and say—in how I live.

Long story short—develop and maintain a living, breathing, speaking, hearing relationship with Father, Son and Holy Ghost. After all, the Kingdom of God is within you and surrounding you ^{Luke 17:21}.

Clothe yourselves therefore, as God's own chosen ones (His own picked representatives), who are purified and holy and well-beloved by God Himself, by putting on behavior marked by tenderhearted pity and mercy, kind feeling, a lowly opinion of yourselves, gentle ways and patience which is tireless and long-suffering, and has the power to endure whatever comes, with good temper. Be gentle and forbearing with one another and, if one has a difference (a grievance or complaint) against another, readily pardoning each other; even as the Lord has freely forgiven you, so must you also forgive.

And above all these put on love and enfold yourselves with the bond of perfectness which binds everything together completely in ideal harmony. And let the peace (soul harmony which comes) from

Christ rule (act as umpire continually) in your hearts deciding and settling with finality all questions that arise in your minds, in that peaceful state to which as members of Christ's one body you were also called to live.

And be thankful (appreciative), giving praise to God always. Let the word spoken by Christ (the Messiah) have its home in your hearts and minds and dwell in you in all its richness, as you teach and admonish and train one another in all insight and intelligence and wisdom in spiritual things, and as you sing psalms and hymns and spiritual songs, making melody to God with His grace in your hearts. And whatever you do (no matter what it is) in word or deed, do everything in the name of the Lord Jesus and in dependence upon His Person, giving praise to God the Father through Him [Colossians 3:12-17].

PREPARATION FOR RESURRECTION

1. To me, love means......
2. If someone really loves me, I expect them to......
3. The way I show love is......
4. What things have happened to me that cause me to withhold love?
5. I don't accept love from some people because......
6. If I allow people to see me as I really am, some people may judge me because......
   - Do I trust God to help me through that?
7. I can move into deeper, more personal relationship with God by......
8. My mentors are:

- I support them by:
- They challenge me by:
9. My protégés are:
  - I promote them by:
  - I challenge them by:

LUKE 10:16

He who hears and heeds you [disciples]
Hears and heeds Me;
And he who slights and rejects you
Slights and rejects Me;
And he who slights and rejects Me
Slights and rejects Him who sent Me.

LUKE 10:19

Behold! I have given you authority and power to trample
upon serpents and scorpions,
and [physical and mental strength and ability]
over all the power that the enemy [possesses];
and nothing shall in any way harm you.

CHAPTER 7
DOMINION

"Dominion is a privilege that carries
great responsibility."

In an earlier chapter I told you we would get back to Dominion. So, here we are.

(I know you know this stuff, but bear with me.)
God said, "Let Us (Father, Son and Holy Spirit) make mankind in Our image, after Our likeness, and let them have complete authority over the fish of the sea, the birds of the air, the tame beasts, and over all the earth and over everything that creeps upon the earth.
*So **God created man in His own image, in the image and likeness of God He created him; male and female He created them*** Genesis 1:26-27.

......For you have stripped off the old (unregenerate) self with its evil practices, and have clothed yourselves with the new spiritual self, **which is ever in the process of being renewed and remolded into fuller and more perfect knowledge upon knowledge after the image (the likeness) of Him Who created it** Colossians 3:9-10

LIKENESS AND IMAGE

Now—sometimes we know things but don't really know them with understanding. How do we get there—what is the next step to understanding?

We see in the above scriptures that God gave mankind dominion over the earth and not only the earth but the surrounding atmosphere and the seas as well as all related stuff. When the woman, Eve, chose to disobey God, believing satan when he told her she wouldn't really die Genesis 3:4-5 rather than what God had said previously, rebellion was birthed in the Earth realm. I find it very interesting that her eyes were not opened to see her nakedness until she gave the fruit to Adam. Then, when both had acted in rebellion, their eyes were opened and they were ashamed. They were both in rebellion, both in disobedience.

They, mankind, in effect, gave up their rights as rulers of earth, they could no longer see God. God's enemy, satan had become "god of this world" 2 Corinthians 4:4, the prince of the power of the air Ephesians 2:2. He knew the people were eternal beings because they had the very breath of God sustaining them. Adam had the authority to kick satan out of the garden, but didn't use it. As a result, satan gained the upper hand and mankind became subject to his rule.

- So, when they believed satan's lie, they lost their immortality, not their eternal nature, becoming mortal with a limited lifespan on earth. There developed a distance (literally) in their relationship with God, and an afterlife separated from Him.
- Not only was mankind affected, all creation began to deteriorate.
  - Mankind no longer had dominion.

When Jesus died on the cross, He redeemed mankind, reclaiming dominion from satan and restoring it to mankind. Through His obedience to the cross, Jesus reinstated mankind's authority even over the one who had ruled earth for thousands of years. He wiped out the penalty of disobedience through His obedience and restored the opportunity for mankind to know and live in communion with God.

The result of the fall was mortal death. Jesus demonstrated His rule over death (hell) and the grave when He rose! So, through obedience to the cross, the consequence of disobedience was nullified. Through His resurrection, death was defeated. Think of the implications of that! Death has already been defeated [Revelation 1:18]. One day it will be destroyed [1 Corinthians 15:26].

When His blood touched earth, creation was redeemed also. The earth could no longer hold the bodies of those righteous who had died and were buried. We are told in Matthew 27:50-53 when Jesus yielded up "the ghost," the veil in the temple was torn from top to bottom, the earth quaked, the rocks shattered and the graves opened—releasing the bodies of the saints who had died and were buried. They went to town and witnessed to many people! This wasn't just one or two people who thought they may have seen a dead person—a ghost. There were "many" who witnessed this awesome miracle.

Earth had to obey the blood of the obedient. We need to get a full revelation of this. Dominion of earth has been returned to us. Watchman Nee in his book, <u>Spiritual Authority</u> states, "Authority is not a matter of outside instruction but of inward revelation." He also reminds us, "The gates of Hades shall not prevail against the church, but a rebellious spirit can open its gates. One reason the church sometimes does not prevail is because of the presence of the rebellious. All sins release the power of death, but the sin of rebellion releases it the most. Only the obedient can shut Hades' gates and <u>release life</u>." Do you see that?!

O.K. Let's get a picture of who we are as the Body of Christ. As I type, my hands obey my mind without rebellion. I think a word and my fingers find the letters that form that word on the keyboard, depress the appropriate keys and the words I think appear on the screen. The same thing happens when I walk. I decide I need something that's on the other side of the room. My legs carry my body toward the object I desire. My feet operate properly without being told what to do, because it's programmed within my system.

We are the body of Christ. If we are in tune with Him Who is our head, whatever needs to be done in our realm of influence to further the Kingdom of Heaven will be done because we obey without question. Our mind, our Head—Jesus Christ, makes a decision and we, His body, carry it out just as our body carries out the desires of our mind.

There are hideous diseases on earth that debilitate our bodies: multiple sclerosis, Hodgkin's, cerebral palsy, muscular dystrophy and several others that cause our bodies to not be able to obey our brain. In effect these diseases cause our bodies to be in rebellion. They paint a dramatic picture of the body of Christ today.

It's as if we are not getting the electrical impulses from our brain, Jesus—our head. And that's exactly what has happened. Rebellion has entered the heart of man and has remained so long that most of us don't even know we're in rebellion. We would know we were disobedient if we could get a revelation of the Word of God.

We can't obey what we don't have the capacity to hear. The capacity to hear is predicated on our knowledge and understanding of the Word of God [Romans 10:17], through which we are able to develop relationship. Even though we are told that the Words of God have gone into all the earth [Psalm 19:1-4; Romans 10:18], and that *the invisible things of Him from the creation of the world are clearly seen, being understood by the things that are made, [even] His eternal power and Godhead; so that they (we) are without excuse* [Romans 1:20]. In other words, we should be able to develop a relationship with the Living God even if we never read a Bible.

While Jesus was here, He taught His followers, not just the twelve, how to walk in dominion. First He sent out the twelve, then he sent seventy others [Luke 10:1-22] to let us, two thousand years later, know that dominion is for all who believe [Mark 16:17-18]. He gave them authority/power over all the power of the enemy; spirits obeyed them, and they rejoiced. Jesus said, "Hey, you're rejoicing about the wrong thing.

115

(That's what is supposed to be going on.) Rejoice because your names are enrolled in heaven."

Behold! I have given you authority and power to trample upon serpents and scorpions, and physical and mental strength and ability over all the power that the enemy possess: and nothing shall in any way harm you. Nevertheless, do not rejoice in this, that the spirits are subject to you but rejoice that your names are enrolled in heaven ^{Luke 10:19-20}.

The word "power" used twice in Luke 10:19 has two distinct meanings. When Jesus gave the disciples "power," that word means, power, authority, right, liberty, jurisdiction and strength. One of numerous possible definitions is "the power of rule or government (the power of Him whose will and commands must be submitted to by others and obeyed) Strong's #1849.

When this same scripture speaks about the power of the enemy, that word means mighty work, strength, miracle, might, and virtue. One of the various possible definitions listed is inherent power, power residing in a thing by virtue of its nature, or which a person or thing exerts and puts forth Strong's #1411.

Look at these two definitively different words and you will see that the "rule of government"—dominion has been given to us by Jesus. By His death, burial, and resurrection, He completely defeated the devil but left us to enforce His victory. It's just like the Children of Israel and the Promised Land. God <u>gave</u> them the Promised Land, but they had to fight to rid that land of the current inhabitants and among them were the giants. Throughout the Bible, God has given us examples of how we are to operate in Earth under His direction.

Now, look at this. This is one of my favorite views of Jesus. In Luke 10:21 we are told……

In that same hour, **He rejoiced and glorified in the** **Holy Spirit** *and said, "I thank You, Father, Lord of heaven and earth, that You have concealed these things (relating to salvation) from the wise and understanding and learned, and revealed them to babes (the childish, unskilled, and untaught). Yes, Father, for such was Your gracious will and choice and good pleasure.*

Can't you just see Jesus rejoicing? Can't you see Him leaping and spinning and gushing in the spirit? Strong's #21–root #242. Oh! I love Jesus! I love thinking of Him rejoicing! I love knowing what brings Him pleasure! I love knowing His passionate personality. I love Him!

It's when we "get it" that He rejoices! And He so wants us to "get it"! These things happened before the cross. After the grave but before the ascension, He confirmed our authority again Mark 16:15-18. But, even more than stated in Mark 16, in Luke 10:21-24, He says, "*All things have been given over into My power by My Father,*" and the Father has chosen to reveal this to the unskilled and untaught. That's us as well as those with Him at that time. All things have been given over to Jesus' power. He is our Head. We are His Body. Therein lies our dominion!

- Dominion is not about our personal power or authority.
- It's about Jesus' power and authority.
- Authority is about obedience.
- Obedience is about relationship.

It isn't that God <u>can't</u> do things on earth simply by sending His thoughts or speaking forth His Word. The current situation is that He has given us a period of time to GET IT! There is appointed a certain period of time wherein mankind has been given dominion on earth and God will work only through mankind to do what needs to be done—sometimes in conjunction with angelic assistance. Not that He couldn't do otherwise. He simply won't go back on His Word. He is not a man that He should lie $^{\text{Numbers } 23:19}$. Besides, He sees the end from the beginning $^{\text{Isaiah } 46:9-10}$. He's outside time and knows how everything is going to work out.

Guess What?! He's trusting us! He's trusting that we will hear and understand and be converted because He has given us the ability to understand the mysteries of the Kingdom of God $^{\text{Luke } 8:10}$! Oh My! Is that WONDERFUL! Wish I could type in tongues that I might glorify and worship God in Spirit and in Truth right here on this paper so <u>you,</u> right there, wherever you are reading this book, could also rejoice, glorifying and worshipping God in Spirit and in Truth!

RELATIONSHIP!

Obedience comes through relationship. Dominion comes through obedience. Remember when Samuel said to Saul, "To obey is better than sacrifice" [1 Samuel 15:22]? Again quoting Watchman Nee from his book <u>Spiritual Authority</u>: "The greatest demand is for (man) to obey. Because even in sacrifice there can be the element of self-will. **Obedience alone is absolutely honoring to God, for it alone takes God's will as its center**. For authority to be expressed there must be subjection. If there is to be subjection, self needs to be excluded; but according to one's self-life, subjection is not possible. **This is only possible when one lives in the Spirit. It is the highest expression of God's will**."

To fulfill our God-given dream, vision, assignment, promise, we will on occasion have to do things that will require us to put aside everything we know or want to do and simply obey. If we could do it in our own wisdom, knowledge and understanding, even adding our own strength, it would already be done. We must have His input. To get His input, we have to hear. To hear demands obedience. Are you hearing what the Spirit is saying? Are you doing what you see the Father do?

Can you sense the impulse—the unction of the Spirit? The Holy Ghost is our connection to the Head. Are you filled with the Holy Spirit? Do you need re-filling? The Word of God demonstrates multiple fillings [Acts 4:8; Acts 13:9; Acts 13:52]. We must be full of His Spirit, His Super on our natural, to fulfill our assignment, do our dream and/or embrace our promise. Every God-given dream is a piece of establishing the Kingdom of Heaven on earth. Doing your God-given dream/ assignment is participating in the Kingdom of God which is in you and around you [Luke 17:21]! Doing your dream is getting the Kingdom, the rule of God, from the inside to the outside to affect change in the earth.

Now, let's look at this. Jesus <u>began</u> to do and teach these things ^{Acts 1:1}, He was the first to do and teach the things He did ^{Strong's #756}. He has authorized us to continue His work until His enemies are made a footstool for His feet ^{1 Corinthians 15:25}. When He said, "It is finished," He was referring to the great mystery, the redemption of mankind and the earth ^{John 19:30; Revelation 10:7}. His part, the fulfilling of His name(s)—all the names that pertain to Jesus including Redeemer, Savior, Bridegroom, Son of Man, Son of God, King of the Earth, King of the Universe, as well as all the other names of Jesus, were fulfilled. His work, the effect of His life, like creation itself, continues being unveiled. Each heart must be redeemed, individually turned to believe His Word.

Be confident that He dwells in us and performs the work through us just as the Father performed the work through Him ^{John 5:19-21; John 14:10}. Your dream or promise is a vital part of that work.

Now look at John 14:12:

......if anyone steadfastly believes in Me, he will himself be able to do the things that I do; and he will do even greater things than these, because I go to the Father. And I will do (I Myself will grant) whatever you ask in My Name (as presenting all that I AM), so that the Father may be glorified and extolled in (through) the Son. Yes, I will grant (I Myself will do for you) whatever you shall ask in My Name (as presenting all that I AM). We're all familiar with that scripture. Now let's tie it together with promises from

the Old Testament. "In the Old the New is concealed. In the New the Old is revealed [Author unknown]. "

*Earnestly remember the former things, which I did of old; for I Am God, and there is no one else; I Am God, and there is none like Me. Declaring the end and the result from the beginning, and from ancient times the things that are not yet done, saying, "My counsel shall stand, and **I will do all My pleasure and purpose*** [Isaiah 46:9-10]. "*

Behold, I am doing a new thing! Now it springs forth; do you not perceive and know it and will you not give heed to it? I will even make a way in the wilderness and rivers in the desert [Isaiah 43:19].

Your God-given dream is part of the "new thing" God is doing. A lot of what's being done today could not have been done before because of the technology required to do it. Your God-given dream plays an integral part in God's plan. Were it not so, He would not have given it to you nor put in your heart a desire to complete it.

Knowing that your authority and dominion rest in your relationship with the Head, Jesus Christ, and that your ability rests in hearing and/or sensing the unctions of Holy Spirit, then responding in obedience can get you on your way.

Do not be anxious and troubled with cares about your life, as to what you will have to eat; or about your body, as to what you will have to wear......Do not be seized with alarm *and struck with fear, little flock, for **it is your Father's good** **pleasure to give you the kingdom*** ^{Luke 12:22 and 32}!

Authority without power is as illusive and ineffectual as a cup of water poured out on the desert
Luke 4:36, 9:1, 24:49

PREPARATION FOR RESURRECTION

1. Rebellion due to ignorance is very subtle. How can I increase knowledge of the Holy—learn to recognize what is holy and the way of holiness so I can walk out of rebellion?
2. How can I submit to Christ more fully so I can walk in dominion in His authority and power?
3. What works of Christ am I willing to commit to being performed through me?
4. In what ways can I participate in a deeper development of relationship with Father, Son, and Holy Spirit?
5. What beliefs and opinions create a short-circuit between me and my "head," Jesus?
6. What relationship in my life has priority over my relationship with my Lord and what do I need to do to change that priority?

CHAPTER 8
PITFALLS, DETOURS, AND DELAYS

"Buried within our souls are hazards to our future that are only revealed by the Light of God's Word."

Jesus' first step into public ministry was at the age of twelve. This was the age young men began being trained in the family trade—they learned their father's business. He knew Who His Father was and He knew what His work was. He had just "come of age," the time He was to "be in His Father's house and occupied about His Father's business" [Luke 2:49]. He knew His Father's business was not carpentry. He knew what His call was. But, the priesthood was not available to Him until He was thirty [Numbers 4:3; 1 Chronicles 23:3]. It wasn't the right season.

Just imagine if you knew what you were called to do and knew how to do it but had to wait eighteen years to get started! Would you go on to something else? Take a different road? Give up and forget about it? Well, for eighteen years Jesus learned to be an excellent carpenter, but He had no problem leaving that role when the time was right.

Maybe that's your deal. If you are fully mature and have no issues, no hurts, no buttons being pushed, maybe it's not the right season. If that's the case, take your lead from Jesus: *And Jesus increased in wisdom (in broad and full understanding) and in stature and years, and in favor with God and man* ^{Luke 2:52}.

Wait for your season. But don't <u>just</u> wait. Increase in wisdom, knowledge and understanding of your assignment. Learn how to have favor with God and man. Get the groundwork laid. Is there specialized or additional training you can obtain? Do you need a business plan? Do you need blueprints? Do you need to be incorporated? Do you need partners? Perhaps you need a grant or a loan. Do everything you can to be ready when the season turns.

Many of us have started "our dream" and for one reason or another let it go.

<u>My personal experience</u>

On November 26, 1999, I was called into full-time ministry. I had been in ministry since 1985 to one degree or another, from having church in our home, to deliverance ministry, intercession, an officer on a local board of an international ministry, and assisting in the formation and operation of a women's outreach through a local church, etc., all the while working full time. I tried to bargain with God:

- I told Him, "In just a few years my retirement will be vested. I'll quit then."
  o He said, "If not now—when?"
- I said, "Well, in just one more year I'll have partial benefits, I'll quit then."
  o He said, "If not now—when?"

- I'll quit at such and such time.
  - He said, "If not now—when?"
- Finally, I said, "I'll quit right after the Christmas holiday."
  - He said, "If not now—when?"
- I said, "O.K.! O.K.! I'll give my notice Monday morning."
- Well. I lasted five months. Money got tight—really tight.
  - Money got out of sight!!!

Of course there were several things I should have done differently. However, I thought I was living/working by faith. Surprise! I really didn't know the first thing about walking in faith. I was "doing" everything I knew to do. I worked really hard and expected that during the process funds would begin coming in. Every day, in every way I knew how, I was "doing my dream." I was fulfilling my call. I didn't ask for strategy. I didn't know to. I prayed a lot, but didn't think to check into what His plans were for finances. I expected my work ethic to carry me and produce the finances I needed. I actually thought that since this was "His" idea, He would make it work.

I felt led to go back to work! Basically, I stepped into disobedience and rebellion—not purposely—ignorantly. For two years, the money that once was plenty, even with increases, no longer stretched far enough. I had attitude problems. I had major sickness. I nearly died. What began as a sinus infection ultimately infected my entire body.

My liver became toxic from a combination of the infection and the medications. My lymphatic system became toxic. I used up all my sick leave. I used most of my vacation. I used sick leave from the corporate pool. My strength was spent. I finally had to go back to work but could only work half a day because I was still so sick and weak. I used the rest of my vacation.

I had so much learning and so little understanding.

For months I really couldn't hear God. I wasn't willing to admit I was so sick. After all, I was "standing on the Word," so I had friends tell my pastor that I was just tired. I finally cried out to God, "Where's my spiritual covering?" While I was yet crying out, the phone rang. It was my Pastor and his wife. He rebuked death from me and released healing to me. Finally, I began healing.

I wanted to pray but I was too tired. I wanted to read the Bible but was unable to concentrate because I was so tired. I continued missing church. Where I lived, I couldn't pull in Christian broadcasting except occasionally on UHF Channels. But TV didn't hold my attention anyway. If I sat down to watch TV, I immediately went to sleep. I began drying up spiritually. I had to do something. So, I began force-feeding myself on the Word. I set schedules when I would pray and read the Bible.

- Before work.
- At 10:00 in the morning—my break time.
- At lunch.
- In the evenings from ASAP till whenever.

I began hearing God again! What was He saying?

- "If not now—when?!"
- "I can take care of you better than you will ever be able to take care of yourself!"

- "Trust Me!"
- "Let me bring restoration into your life!"
- "Trust Me!"

There came a time my pastor spoke a word to the general assembly. The same word was given following service three Sunday's in a row. Each Sunday, Pastor specified that it was not for everyone, but those for whom it was would know. He said, "You have been called into full time ministry and because you won't leave your comfort zone and step into your call, God is going to have the companies you work for to go bankrupt."

At first I did not believe this could be for me. I think I got "confirmation" five or six different times. I worked for the state and had heard nothing of state bankruptcy. Guess What!? Monday after the third Sunday, I discovered the state was "in dire financial straits" and the institution I was working for had to reduce staff by one third! I immediately turned in my resignation.

It's scary to go some place you've already failed. I simply wasn't sure I was trustworthy. But I knew the message was for me. The last time I insisted on one more confirmation, it came from my pastor <u>after</u> I had given my notice at work. I hadn't shared my plans with him. He really hears God and I sort of (really) wanted God to tell him. God doesn't hide anything from him, so why not tell him this so I could have my treasured confirmation? So, the Sunday after I had given my notice on Friday, the Word of the Lord came through my pastor to me.

It was after the evening service and there were about a half-dozen of us standing around. Pastor began speaking prophetically to each one. I was the last. Several things were spoken to me punctuated with, "Thus saith the Lord, 'If you'll take care of My business, I'll take care of your business.'" I suspect that was said as many times as I had insisted on confirmation that I had heard God.

Well, I've been in full time ministry for a number of years now. It got pretty scary a time or two, but He has been faithful. Please understand. I'm not suggesting anyone follow my lead. You have to hear God for yourselves. But I can tell you—God is faithful. He won't ask you to do anything He's not willing and well able to equip you for......

- Physically.
- Emotionally.
- Experientially.
- Financially.

Certainly, there were and still are tough times. I still had a lot to learn—still do. Sometimes I limit God, in various ways. Sometimes I get ahead of Him. Sometimes I drag behind. Are there tests and trials? Yes. Do I pass them all? No. But, I know He has called me, appointed me, anointed me, and equipped me. He has proven Himself faithful over and over again. In every situation, He is ready and willing to give me His best.

There is one more thing we must discuss here. It's something we hear very little about, but you find it in Scripture. Vexation of spirit.

- Deuteronomy 28:20, Vexation means "tumult, confusion, disquietude, turmoil, discomfiture, destruction, trouble, disturbance, panic, vexed, vexation ^{Strong's #1949}."

- Ecclesiastes 1, 2, 4, and 6, it means "longing, striving ^{Strong's 7469},"

- Isaiah 9:1, it means "constraint, and distress ^{Strong's 4164},"

- Isaiah 28:19, vexation means "a horror, an object of terror, a trembling, an object of trembling ^{Strong's #2113},"

- Isaiah 65:14, it's a word that means "breaking, fracture, crushing, breach, crash, ruin, shattering ^{Strong's #7667},"

Oh, my! This is a place—a time—a condition that causes you to feel imprisoned and impotent. You can't figure out what is holding you back. You can't move forward. You've done everything you know to do. You've repented, fasted, prayed, and made positive declaration. Yet—still—you're held captive. You hear God. You aren't in sin that you're aware of, but you can't move forward. And—there are issues you can't seem to get past. This is what's called vexation of spirit.

Vexation of spirit often requires deliverance. Many times, vexation of spirit is anchored in your past. Perhaps generational. Maybe relational. It could be soul ties—even ones you've broken several times. You need help. Seek counsel. There may be several books on this subject, but one I'm familiar with and highly recommend is—Time to Defeat The Devil by Chuck Pierce. In this book Dr. Pierce addresses vexation of spirit as well as several other things that keep us bound.

Study the life of David:

- Anointed to <u>be</u> king as a teenager.
- Finding his way to the throne—his appointed place, through years in the School of the Spirit.
- Running and hiding from the reigning king.
- Living in caves.
- Often going hungry.
- One time he pretended to be crazy and hid out in the enemy's territory.
- Still, he prevailed and God set him on the throne of Judah and Israel—uniting the nation.

So, whatever you do, if you know your call, promise, dream, assignment, or at least that you were put here for **some** kind of purpose—Never Give Up!

PREPARATION FOR RESURRECTION

1. What are some of the areas/things wherein I failed to one degree or another?
2. What have I learned through these experiences?
3. What have I learned that I need deeper understanding to operate in fully?
4. Am I using my faith or trusting in my abilities?
5. How am I improved spiritually?
6. How am I better equipped:
   - Physically?
   - Emotionally?
   - Experientially?
   - Financially?
7. Does my passion match or surpass my potential?

- If so, how can I focus that passion to utilize its energy to accomplish my dream?
- If not, what can I do to become passionate enough to overcome past failures?

8. Am I committed enough to do something toward my dream every day?
   - If so, what are some of the things I can do to work toward my goal?
   - If not, what is my **real** dream or promise?

1 TIMOTHY 3:16

. . . great and important and weighty, we confess, is the
hidden truth (the mystery, secret) of godliness.
He (God) was made visible in human flesh,
Manifested and vindicated in the Holy Spirit,
Was seen by angels,
Believed on in the world,
And
Taken up in glory

CHAPTER 9
KNOWING JESUS

"Knowing about Him is not enough.
Not enough for you.
Not enough for Him.
He really wants a personal relationship with you."

There are some other things we can examine. For one thing—don't limit God! Look at the Children of Israel.

How oft did they provoke Him in the wilderness, [and] grieve Him in the desert! Yea, they turned back and tempted God, and **limited** *the Holy One of Israel*
Psalm 78:40-41 KJV

- Limited ^{Strong's #8428}:
  - o To pain, wound, trouble, cause pain

Oh, My! Is that where I fit?! I already know I have limited Him in various ways and times. Have I grown past that or do I still limit Him, cause Him pain, wound or trouble Him?

Nothing is impossible with God. You must learn to fully trust Him. If you know He's called you and you don't consider yourself to be well enough equipped or, like me, not sure you're trustworthy—He will enable you. Stick with it. Stick with Him and His plan for your life.

He tells us in Luke 14:26 that if we don't hate our father, mother, wife (husband) and children as well as our brothers and sisters, even our own life in comparison to how much we love Him we cannot be His disciples, His followers. We must give Him first place. His plan is best for us and for everyone with whom we have to do. Trust Him. Listen. Then obey.

Here's another thing. You don't have to wait till you get to heaven to reap rewards. There will be rewards in heaven but hear what He has to say about here and now:

Anyone and everyone who has left houses or brothers or sisters or father or mother or children or lands for My Name's sake will receive many (even a hundred) times more and will inherit eternal life Matthew 19:29.

One more thing about rewards. Don't let pride or a religious spirit rob you of anything The Lord wants to give you. It's a little like when you buy a car or a house. It isn't just the shell—it will have windows, doors, lights, etc. God's plan for us is like that. Included in what He wants from us is what He wants to give us. Just in case there are still questions about what that means, Mark records it more clearly, a little different verbiage.

Jesus said, "Truly I tell you, there is no one who has given up and left house or brothers or sisters or

*mother or father or children or lands for My sake and for the Gospel's **who will not receive a hundred times as much now in this time**—houses and brothers and sisters and mothers and children and lands, with persecutions—and in the age to come eternal life"*
Mark 10:29-30
.

These choices are hard to make and shouldn't even be considered unless you know in our heart you have heard God and He requires such choices of you.

Of course, changes are going to have to be made. Good habits are so hard to form and so easy to lose! Your flesh rebels—you have to kill it. Satan tries to interfere—you have to exclude his voice. Wanting and wishing can't get you where you really need to be. If you don't put action to it, you won't make it. Change is not easy, but it is worth it.

If you are hanging on to SELF......

- This is the way I am.
- I've always been this way.
- My grandparents were this way and it's good enough for me.
  - o Then you are preventing Christ from being fully formed in you.
  - o You are limiting God just as surely as the children of Israel did and were not permitted to enter the Promised Land first time around.
    - God didn't keep them out.
      - They kept themselves out!

Paul says in Galatians 4:19:

*My little children, for whom I am again suffering birth pangs **until Christ is completely and permanently formed (molded) within you.***

Peter states in 2 Peter 1:4:
*By means of these (His glory and excellence) He has bestowed on us His precious and exceedingly great promises, so that through them you may escape (by flight) from the moral decay (rottenness and corruption) that is in the world because of covetousness (lust and greed), and **become sharers (partakers) of the divine nature.***

It isn't just about you and me. It's about Christ and His body. It's about the future of mankind and eternity. And He's so determined that we make it. Christ is currently being formed in us by Holy Spirit so we can partake of the divine nature! We should do everything we can to not alienate ourselves from Him. We need to really get to know Him.

Now, to have knowledge of a thing and to really know it are two different things. Proverbs tells us in Chapter 4 verse 7:

The beginning of Wisdom is: get Wisdom (skillful and godly Wisdom)! For skillful and godly Wisdom is the principal thing. And with all you have gotten, get understanding (discernment, comprehension and interpretation).

To really know something is to have it active and working in your life. We may study something for years and think we know it. But, until the fruit is evident in our life, we don't really know it. We need to really get to know Jesus and let Christ be formed in us so the out-workings of His Spirit are evident in our lives.

Allowing Holy Spirit to begin bearing His fruit in our life, makes evident His indwelling presence through the manifestation of His character:

- Love
- Joy
- Peace
- Patience (an even temper, forbearance)
- Kindness
- Goodness (benevolence)
- Faithfulness
- Gentleness (meekness, humility)
- Self-Control (self-restraint, continence) [Galatians 5:22-23].

These are not characteristics we can develop of our own effort. They are outgrowths of Christ being formed in us through the indwelling of Holy Spirit.

When we read the Word of God, "name" actually means "everything which the name conveys, everything the thought or feeling of which is aroused in the mind by mentioning, hearing, remembering, the name, i.e., for one's rank, authority, interests, pleasure, command, excellences, deeds, etc." [STRONG'S #3686].

This is the "knowing," the understanding we have of Him that backs up our prayers when we say, "In the name of Jesus."

- By what name(s) do you know Jesus?
- Do you really know Him as Redeemer?

137

- Do you actually know Him as Savior?
- How about Husband, Healer, Conquering King, Provider, Mentor, Brother, Messiah?
- What experience or expression of His character comes to your mind when you speak His name?
  - Prince of Peace, Holy One, Creator of the Universe?
- Do you think of Him as Child, the Babe in the Manger, The Crucified, or The Risen?
- Do you know Him as Way-Maker, Righteous Judge, Advocate, Intercessor?
- Do you know Him as Friend?

There are so many "ways" to know our Lord. The more we get to know Him, the more Christ is formed in us and the more we look like Him and even smell like Him.

Smell? YES! Many people have expressed their experience of the aroma of His presence. Some smell roses. Others smell a "sweet" fragrance. Some smell spice of one type or another, often cinnamon even myrrh. I have smelled these things but normally I smell what the Spirit conferred to me as "Creation." It's an inexpressible fragrance that refreshes and carries peace, joy, and comfort. It causes me to stop—smile—rejoice. It carries me by the Spirit into His manifest presence.

Often, the fragrance we smell during times of ministry, teaching, worship, etc., is representative of the anointing on the minister. It reveals the relationship of that minister with the Lord.

*But thanks be to God, Who in Christ always leads us in triumph as trophies of Christ's victory and **through us spreads and makes evident the fragrance of the knowledge of God everywhere*** ^{2 Corinthians 2:14}.

Knowing Him is worth any price. Paul says in Philippians 3:7 that what he once considered gain (beneficial) he now (after getting to know Christ) considered loss—a waste. After all, in Him we live and move and have our being for we are His offspring ^{Acts 17:28}. Many have given their lives for knowing Him. Throughout the world even today, martyrdom is increasing in non-Christian nations. People are being killed because of their relationship with Him. Would you die rather than deny Him? Would I?

Please note: Martyrdom is not "killing yourself." Rather it is the suffering of death on account of adherence to a cause and especially to one's religious faith ^{www.merriam-ebster.com/dictionary/martyrdom}. For Christians, martyrdom is when someone kills you to prevent Christ's influence through you toward other people. That's what laying down your life is—being willing to die if necessary to fulfill your call. I know of no instance in the Word of God when He asked someone to end their mortal life for Him. No! Instead He gave His life for us! He wants us to **live** for Him.

GET TO KNOW JESUS!

For my determined purpose is that I may know Him (that I may progressively become more deeply and intimately acquainted with Him perceiving and recognizing and understanding the wonders of His Person more strongly and more clearly), and that I may in that same way come to know the power out-

flowing from His resurrection which it exerts over believers, and that I may so share His sufferings as to be continually transformed in sprit into His likeness even to His death, in the hope that if possible I may attain to the spiritual and moral resurrection that lifts me out from among the dead even while in the body. Not that I have now attained this ideal, or have already been made perfect, but I press on to lay hold of (grasp) and make my own, that for which Christ Jesus (the Messiah) has laid hold of me and made me His own ^{Philippians 3:10-12}.

Do you know Him – really know Him?

Even if we do really know Him, there is so much more to learn about Him and so many more ways to really know Him.
He is the Ancient of Days.
In Him we live and move and have our being.
He is the One Who was and is and is to come!

PREPARATION FOR RESURRECTION
1. What am I willing to "die" to in order to live more fully in Him?
2. What am I not willing to let go of that I may pursue Him?
3. How am I limiting God?
4. By what name(s) do I know the Lord?
   - Not, how many names of the Lord do I know?
   - **Rather,** He is real to me in the ways these names represent.

CHAPTER 10
WEALTH AND PROSPERITY

"You can't do your dream without finances,
But
Without godly character
Both
Dreams and finances will fail."

Let's look at wealth. What is it and what is it not?

Wealth is so much more than money. We need to have a prosperous soul, prosperous relationships, prosperous mind, prosperous projects. If you don't think you can handle wealth, even if you've proven in the past that you can't, ask God to change you. Ask Him to reveal what needs to be changed in you so that you can properly handle prosperity. It may be generational. It may be your personal experience. It may be a curse or a "mis-belief." Find out what keeps you from moving into prosperity. You may even need to find out why you don't want to be prosperous.

You may not want wealth but God wants you to have it. In effect, when we resist wealth, we are fighting against God. Look at this:

But you shall earnestly remember the Lord your God,
*for **it is He Who gives you power to get wealth that***
***He may establish His covenant** which He swore to*
your fathers, as it is this day ^{Deuteronomy 8:18}.

It looks like to some degree the establishing of God's covenant is dependent upon us gaining wealth in all areas of our lives through the power He has given us. When we attain success, wealth, prosperity, it encourages our friends and relatives to press toward believing they can do better as well. I know. Some of our friends and relatives will ridicule us as they do in anything we attempt to be different from status quo. But if they have an opportunity, they certainly don't turn their backs on it. Suddenly, their whole attitude changes and they have HOPE!

Let's look at some of the words in the above scripture. Now, the word "get" ^{Strong's #6213}, has several possible definitions including:

- To work
- To do
- To obtain
- To obtain property
- To press
- To squeeze.

O.K., let's look at the word "wealth." There are several Hebrew and Greek words translated as "wealth."

- Strength, might, efficiency, wealth, army, and/or ability ^{Strong's #2428}.
- Pleasant, agreeable (to the senses), (to the higher nature), excellent (of its kind), rich, valuable in

estimation, glad, happy, good understanding (of man's intellectual nature), prosperous (of man's sensuous nature), kind, benign, good, right (ethical), moral good, benefit, welfare, prosperity, happiness, good things (collective), bounty [Strong's 2896].

- To accumulate (riches, treasures) [Strong's #5233].
- Wealth, riches, substance, enough!, sufficiency [Strong's 1952].
- Multiply, increase, become many, etc. [Strong's 7235].
- Strength, power, might of God, angels, and animals [Strong's 3581].
- Riches, means, wealth [Strong's 2142].

Word studies are so interesting! You might enjoy the root of "wealth" [Strong's #2342].

- To twist, whirl about, dance, writhe, fear, tremble, travail, be in anguish, be pained, suffer torture, wait longingly.

WOW! That's something to wrap yourself around. Pause and think on that!

And here's something that may be a surprise to a few. "Get" can also mean "to make an offering." Don't ever leave out giving. If there is one most important thing about getting, it's giving. Many of us have a problem with the thought of giving to get. However, we expect to have to plant seeds to get a garden. And, if we plant seeds for a garden, we do everything we can to make sure we get a crop, whether flowers, grass or food.

Why should we think differently about anything else we need? We barter with one another. "I'll give you this and this if you'll give me that." "I'll do this for you if you'll do that for me." Same principle. As a matter of fact, money is a seed we use to get what we want or need. Everything works by seed. Don't short-change yourself because you are unwilling to get the Kingdom view of seedtime and harvest. Study it out in God's Word. A good place to begin is Genesis 8:22.

I had an awesome revelation some years ago. I was really pressing into the things of God. Some of my friends and family thought I had become delusional because the revelations I was getting did not fit the doctrine of our denomination. At that time I did not have access to many television channels, so I did not know what the Lord was releasing to others. The Spirit showed me how Jesus was planted in the earth like a seed [John 12:24] because God wanted a family. When Jesus died on the cross then was buried and rose, He became "the first fruits, first begotten of the dead, firstborn among many brethren" [1 Corinthians 15:23, Revelation 1:5, Romans 8:29]. It is the ultimate demonstration of seed time and harvest.

A while after I had this awesome revelation, I began hearing other ministers saying it as well. God wanted a family so He planted His Son. You see, because there is only one Spirit and only one Body, when the Spirit speaks revelation, the Body hears it. The listening ear hears [Matthew 11, 13; Mark 4, 7; Luke 8, 14; Revelation 2-3]. None of us have an exclusive on anything pertaining to God. His Word is not for private interpretation [2 Peter 1:20]. Those who have an ear to hear—hear [Revelation 2:7,11,17,29; 3:6,13, 22]. He's no respecter of persons, so when He gives us a dream, there are others out there dreaming it as well. We can try to do it by ourselves, or we can hook up with others in our dream family, our vision and calling family, and work together for Kingdom purposes. However, the first thing we need to do is ask Holy Spirit how to proceed.

So, He's not telling us we don't have to work for wealth. We may have to work hard, press and squeeze to get it, both physically and characteristically, but He does want us to have it. We may have to change attitudes, geographic locations, friends. We may have to obtain more education and/or training. During our "getting" we may have to do some "doing without" so we can invest time, money and effort toward our goal. It will be worth it.

Now, I'm not talking about just getting rich. You will never be happy just being rich. But, if you develop godly character and build your wealth on godly principles, you will attain both prosperity in every area of your life, and happiness to boot.

The best, quickest, and safest way to get is to give. Seed into people who are doing their dream. Seed into people who carry the anointing you have or desire. Seed into people who God appoints to further your strength and power. Sometimes the currency of giving is related to time, energy, talents/skills, compassion, etc. Money is not the only currency to use on your way to wealth.

- Don't forget to give to the widow and orphan and take care of the poor.
- Don't fail to tithe and give First Fruits.

Just giving without being led of the Spirit is not seeding. Giving everywhere you perceive a need is not seeding. As Jesus said in Matthew 26, Mark 4, and John 12, we'll always have the poor with us. Sometimes wealth is assigned for specific things that actually help a greater number of people when properly applied to inventions, books, investments, etc. Give as the Spirit of the Living God directs and it will produce a harvest for you and the soil you sow into. Be sure that in your giving you don't give away the assignment He gave you the wealth to accomplish.

If you don't have money, give what you have. Your time is the most valuable commodity on earth. You have been appointed a specified amount of time. You have to spend it wisely. You can make more money, buy more land and get more material stuff. You can't make more time. Sow some time. Sow what you sow wisely.

There are several really good authors who have written about finances. I recommend Robert Mawire, Oral Roberts, Kenneth Copeland, Mark Davis, Jerry Tuma, Mike Murdock, Kenneth Hagin, Larry Burkett, John Avanzini, Pat Francis, and there are many others.

Please understand, these people deal with character building along with wealth getting. Money without godly character is destructive and will harm you and those around you as well. Work on YOU while you work on finances. Develop wealth in every area of your life, every relationship. Develop a wealth of knowledge, understanding, and wisdom which gives you the ability to apply that knowledge and understanding.

One more thing on this subject. We must allow others to seed into our lives. God made us to prosper—to multiply. To deny the need for finances, favor, or opportunity, and to deny Him the pleasure of rewarding us is normally an indication of infestation of a religious spirit. When we refuse to accept/receive help from people, we deny them the privilege of seed time and harvest. We deny them the opportunity to multiply and be blessed by their giving. Giving to us may be the key that unlocks financial breakthrough for them. If we can't receive what mere man can offer us, what will we do with the gifts offered by God.

PREPARATION FOR RESURRECTION

1. How do I define wealth?
2. What are my true feelings/beliefs about money?
3. Do I get angry toward ministers who ask for money or who look like they have too much?
   - If so, make a list of those ministers and look behind the scenes. Find out what they do with their money besides what you can see.
     - Do they support an orphanage, feed children, train people in third world countries how to make a living, train ministers and send them forth?
     - Also find out where their money comes from.
       - Do they have books, CD's, DVD's, they sell? Perhaps they have investments or an inheritance. Their wealth may not have anything to do with the church.
   - The issue may be related to your idea of how men and women of God should live—in poverty, dependent on handouts, kept humble to preserve their piety. If so, the real issue may be in your misunderstanding of God's plan for His servants.
     - Don't neglect this search. Your attitude toward those with wealth can affect your ability to gain and/or sustain wealth.
4. What are the benefits of living in lack?

5. What are the benefits of having more than enough?
6. What character issues do I need to work on to handle finances properly?
7. How much of my understanding of wealth can I back up with scripture.

CHAPTER 11
FINAL REVIEW

"Is this what God wants to do through me,
Or
Is this what I want to do for Him?"

Not every dream, vision or desire of your heart is from God. In 2 Samuel 7 and 1 Chronicles 17, we read how David loved God so much he wanted to build a house where God's name/presence could dwell. When he told his dream, his desire to Nathan the prophet, Nathan said, "Do all that is in your heart to do because God is with you."

In the night God spoke to Nathan and said, "I didn't tell David to build Me a house. He is a bloody man and I have appointed one of his sons to build me a house" (paraphrased).

David wasn't offended when he learned God did not want him to build Him a house. God had appointed David to subdue the nations, take dominion and set up a godly government. He was also appointed to bring forth a son who would walk in wisdom and understanding. One who had not been involved in the seasons of war. One who was not a bloody man.

No, David was not offended. He was still excited. He began gathering everything Solomon would need. He contacted kings in other countries and had gold, fine linen, cedar wood, iron, brass—everything that would be needed to build God's house brought to Jerusalem. He stockpiled everything that would be needed to complete the temple including materials for the utensils, the pots and pans, the curtains. Everything [1 chronicles 27, 28]. 1 Chronicles 23-25 tells us King David even set up the government and running of the house of God. But he did not build the house.

We can see how important it is to know if what we purpose to do is in God's plan for our life or if it's simply something we want to do for Him, others or for even ourselves.

Some Dreams Need To Die:

Author's Note: It is of utmost importance to have your dream or vision, renewed, updated, or revised according to God's plan for you at this time in your life. At one point the Children of Israel missed God, refusing to enter the Promised Land because of the report of 10 of the 12 sent to spy out the land. When they later decided to do what He had asked it was too late and they were beaten, crushed by the Canaanites [Numbers 14:26-45]. All those of the generation that was rescued from Egypt but refused to take the promise in its season, died in the wilderness except Joshua and Caleb. The children of those who died lived the promise 40 years later.

The gifts and callings of God are irrevocable [Romans 11:29]. Yet, there is a season, an appointed time for everything. You can't make a thing successful before its time. Nor can you make it happen when its' time has passed. If you've been resisting God's plan for your life, repent quickly! Seek His mercy. Ask Him what needs to be done to get back on track. Then do what He says.

Make a list of your dreams, your promises, your life plan. Pray over each item listed asking yourself these questions:

- Is this an "Iwannabe" or does it fit into God's plan for my life?
- Is this what other people have expected of me from my youth?
- Is this what people expect of me now?
- Is this part of God's plan for my life at this time?

Develop a new list from what is left. Then, pray and ask God to reveal to you the order in which to proceed.

Once you establish your long range goals, develop short range goals to take you to your expected end. Each of these lists requires much prayer.

Don't fall into the trap of a goal without vision to attain. Without vision people perish ^{Proverbs 29:18}. Vision requires prophetic insight and declarations spoken directly to you by God or through a trusted prophetic voice in your life. It is important you hear from God for yourself but also important to gather advice from many counselors ^{Proverbs 11:14}.

A God given dream is often not what is commonly called "ministry." Your dream may require you to be His godly representative in the market places of the world or within your own community.

For those of us who are required to leave what we call "secular employment," it is often difficult to move from the comfort zone and seeming security of a regular paycheck from a 9 to 5 job to aggressively pursuing our ministry goals, even though the Lord, Himself, told us to do so. The violent take the Kingdom of Heaven by force:

> . . . *From the days of John the Baptist until the present time, the kingdom of heaven has endured violent assault, and violent men seize it by force as a precious prize—a share in the heavenly kingdom is sought with most ardent zeal and intense exertion* Matthew 11:12.

You rarely get what you don't pursue.
- When or if you do get something without pursuit you can only keep it by pursuing.
- Normally when we get something we didn't pursue:
  o We don't want it.
  o Don't appreciate it.
  o Don't know how to keep it
    ▪ Let alone cultivate it.

You may have to leave people, places and things. If you are around people who don't believe in you, they will pull you down. Often, they don't want you to change because they, themselves, are not ready to change. They may try to prevent you from moving forward through guilt:
- If you love me . . . .
- If you REALLY love me . . .
- Who do you think you are?
- You think you're better than everyone else!

They may actually become your enemy, in effect holding you hostage so they can remain comfortable. That's not love.

Often the Lord will pull you up by the roots and plant you someplace else. Geographical change may be necessary to step into your God given destiny. Geographical change......

- Takes you out of your comfort zone.
- Takes you away from distracting influences.
- Causes you to connect with new influences:
  - New people.
  - New habits.
  - New determination to succeed.
  - Deeper faith.
  - Greater confidence.
  - Greater reliance on the Lord.

Some things won't fit in your future:
- You may no longer have time to go boating every weekend.
- You may not have time to build model airplanes or fix jigsaw puzzles.
- You may not have time to maintain your yard the way you want.
- Video games may be taking up too much of your time.
- Maybe the TV has to go!
- It may be necessary to replace some of these things with fitness and health.
  - o Pursuing your dream or ministry requires strength and endurance.

SET A GUARD ON . . .

- Heart
- Thoughts
- Mouth
- Eyes
- Ears

If you have confirmed that your dream, vision, promise is from God's heart to yours, count the cost, then proceed with the help of prayer, prophetic insight and many counselors.

If you have received prophetic words, use them as weapons against the enemies of passivity, doubt, fear, and unbelief.

Every day, do something toward making your dream a reality and stepping into your promise.

PREPARATION FOR RESURRECTION

1. Am I ready to commit to continued work on myself and my dreams?
2. What dreams, visions, promises are of my own choosing rather than God's plan?
3. What is God's plan for my life?
4. What promises has He made to me, personally?
5. What is my part in bringing these promises to pass"
6. What dreams, visions, promises do I need to call forth now, at this time?

CHAPTER 12
THE KEY TO THE LAZARUS GENERATION

This chapter is for those who have examined their dreams and determined they are God-given. You've worked on yourself and made a commitment to God and to yourself to continue maturing—developing godly character.

Now, it's time to follow "The Law of New Life." John 12:24 tells us:

I assure you, most solemnly I tell you, Unless a grain of wheat falls into the earth and dies, it remains just one grain; it never becomes more but lives by itself alone. But if it dies, it produces many others and yields a rich harvest.

- **LAZARUS:**
  - He was in the grave four days!
    - He was stinking!
      - WHAT HAPPENED?!
      - JESUS CALLED HIM FORTH!

- NEW LIFE HAPPENED!

Many souls came into the Kingdom of God because of Lazarus' death. He was a grain of wheat that produced much life.

Is your Lazarus—your dream stinking yet?
- **JESUS**
  - He was in the grave three days!
    - The hope of mankind—gone!
      - WHAT HAPPENED?

NEW LIFE HAPPENED!

LET'S LOOK AT THOSE DRY BONES!

Ezekiel 37:1-10:
The hand of the Lord was upon me, and He brought me out in the Spirit of the Lord and set me down in the midst of the valley; and it was full of bones. And He caused me to pass round about them, and behold, there were very many (human bones) in the open valley or plain, and behold they were very dry.

WALK THROUGH YOUR DREAMS!
IF THEY ARE NOT DRY—VERY DRY—THEY
MAY NOT BE DEAD ENOUGH!

And He said to me, "Son of man, can these bones live?" and I answered, "O Lord God, You know!" Again He said to me, "Prophesy to these bones and say to them, 'O you dry bones, hear the word of the

Lord. Thus says the Lord God to these bones: Behold,
I will cause breath and spirit to enter you, and you
shall live; and I will lay sinews upon you and bring
flesh upon you and cover you with skin, and I will put
breath and spirit in you and you (dry bones) shall
live; and you shall know, understand, and realize that
I am the Lord (the Sovereign Ruler), <u>Who calls forth</u>
<u>loyalty and obedient service.</u>'"

So I prophesied as I was commanded; and as I
prophesied, there was a thundering noise and behold
a shaking and trembling and a rattling, and the bones
came together, bone to its bone. And I looked and
behold, there were sinews upon the bones and flesh
came upon them and skin covered them over, but
there was no breath or spirit in them.

Then said He to me, "Prophesy to the breath and
spirit, son of man and say to the breath and spirit,
'Thus says the Lord God: come from the four winds,
O breath and spirit, and breathe upon these slain that
they may live.'"

So I prophesied as He commanded me, and the breath
and spirit came into the bones, and they lived and
stood upon their feet, an exceedingly great host.

Then He said to me, "Son of man, these bones are the
whole house of Israel. Behold, they say, Our bones
are dried up and our hope is lost; we are completely
cut off. Therefore prophesy and say to them, "Thus

says the Lord God: Behold, I will open your graves and cause you to come up out of your graves, O My people; and I will bring you back home to the land of Israel. And you shall know that I am the Lord (your Sovereign ruler), When I have opened your graves, O My people. And I shall put My Spirit in you and you shall live, and I shall place you in your own land. Then you shall know, understand, and realize that I the Lord have spoken it and performed it,'" says the Lord.

BELOVED—IT'S TIME TO PROPHESY TO THE DEAD BONES OF YOUR GOD GIVEN DREAMS.

- CALL THEM FORTH.
- CALL LIFE INTO THEM.
- CALL BREATH INTO THEM
- NEVER GIVE UP!!!

CALL ON

THE

WIND OF THE SPIRIT

TO BLOW ON THE DRY BONEOS

OF YOUR DREAMS

YOUR VISION

YOUR CALL

RESURRECTION DECLARATION

HEAR ME YOU DRY BONES!

**DREAM, VISION,
ASSIGNMENT, CALLING!**

YOU SHALL LIVE AND NOT DIE!

**I CALL YOU TO FULLNESS OF
LIFE AND PURPOSE!**

MY HOPE IS RENEWED!

MY STRENGTH IS RESTORED!

I SHALL OVERCOME!

I SHALL SUCCEED!

IN THE NAME OF JESUS CHRIST OF NAZARETH,

BY THE POWER OF HIS SPIRIT,

AND FOR HIS KINGDOM'S SAKE.

AMEN—SO BE IT!

ABOUT THE AUTHOR

VELMA CROW—Ordained and Licensed Minister, Founder and President of the Ministry Network; Co-Founder and President of Wisdom Merchants. Velma is an anointed, experienced conference speaker and teacher who flows in the Spirit often addressing issues with the skill of a trained surgeon with words of wisdom and words of knowledge. She operates in the seer gift and is dedicated to assisting in the revealing of the Sons of God and establishing His Kingdom on earth.

Velma's heart is to be used in propagating knowledge of the Living God and life in the Spirit, establishing skillful and godly wisdom in those around her.

Her messages draw you into a more intimate relationship with God and give you a hunger for that tangible relationship with His ever present Spirit. She has a heart for releasing others to love and live in the fullness of their God given future and purpose.

On a number of occasions, Velma has presented a seminar entitled "The Death, Burial and Resurrection of Your Dreams" on which this book is based.

Look for other books by Velma such as, <u>Revelation of Visitation</u>. She is also building a discipleship series entitled, <u>Understanding for the New Believer</u>. Look for her book, <u>Psalms From The Secret Place</u>.

To schedule Velma to come to your area you may contact her at <u>admin@wisdommerchants.org</u>.

www.ingramcontent.com/pod-product-compliance
Lightning Source LLC
Chambersburg PA
CBHW072006040426
42447CB00009B/1507